Midlife
Is NOT
A Crisis

Rediscover Your Drive
& Reclaim Your Happiness

To my ancestors.
With love and gratitude.

CONTENTS

ACKNOWLEDGMENTS

This book has been a long time in the making!

Through my own journey of life, I have learned much, gained much and hopefully, given in return in equal measure.

There are so many people who have supported me, too many to mention by name, but there are a few to whom I wanted to give special mention:

Marie Nangle, who has been an incredible lady and taught my daughters and me so much about love and giving, thank you from the bottom of my heart.

My two daughters, Laura and Sarah, for their unfailing support no matter how much of a pickle I got myself into; they were right there cheering me on. Words really cannot convey how much that has meant to me, but you know. Love you to the moon and back!

Wendy Makepeace Browne, my best friend and a real inspirational force in the world! She has an amazing outlook on life, trusting and believing in people as well as herself. She set me on the path of self-forgiveness and trusting and believing in myself when we met in 2004 – a friend in every sense of the word and one I would drop everything for – always there.

Jo Hughes, a very good friend who was the

first person who noticed my potential and actively sought me to join a management training programme which boosted by self-confidence and goes above and beyond. You taught me so many practical approaches to work and life and they have sustained me ever since – you star you!

Kia Bing-Davies – my coach and friend, without whom I would not be where I am today. She has helped reframe my doubts, boosted the successes in my life and provided me with a whole new refreshing energy that I didn't believe I had. Love and light to you sweetheart.

Blackcard Books and Gerry Roberts – for starting me on this amazing journey! I wouldn't be where I am now if it was not for your encouragement, and guidance at the beginning of my journey.

Lyn Thurman at the Quiet Rebel Bureau publishing house – for turning up in my world to help me through my confusion and frustration – published at last!

And finally, last but by no means least! Those wonderful people who have shown themselves to be my quiet advocates; Tess Bates, Andrew Sansom and Heather Spencer for proof reading this book and giving such valuable feedback, Nick Keir for helping me to start on the promotional trail and Debbie Loveridge always there supporting me when I need it! Thank you so much for your love and support.

PREFACE

This book came about as a result of my own Midlife challenges and yes, you can have more than one if you do not heed the signs!

I have spent nearly 20 years working through the various aspects of my life that I was unhappy with, and like most people covered love, money, relationships and health.

When I started out, there was very little in the way of self-help books that address mind, body, emotions and spirit. Midlife is NOT a Crisis aims to provide that balance.

Having worked with clients over time experiencing similar issues to me (the big questions such as who am I? What am I doing? Where am I going? Emotions such as overwhelm, loss, stress and anxiety) it became clear to me that there was a need for a self-help book that really did offer self-help.

Midlife is NOT a Crisis is based around the model I used in my therapy practice which has proven to be very effective and fast acting, by helping the reader to begin to understand who they really are, as opposed to who they have become. The inner you is waiting to be heard and healed.

I am not perfect, I am just like you and I share with you the exercises in this book that I still use and I believe can help you too.

CHAPTER 1
INTRODUCTION

Have you ever looked at yourself in the mirror and wondered who was looking back at you?

Do you wonder what happened to that bright young thing you were with all the hopes and dreams to strive for?

Do you feel like life has become too stressful and demanding, with no you time?

Lost yourself in the humdrum of life and beginning to realise that you feel dead inside and just going through the motions of living?

Feeling exhausted?

Me too!

I was 36.

Wake-Up Call #1

I was splitting up with my husband. It was a difficult time for us both; we had debts, two young children and we both had demanding jobs. Plus, we both had issues we were not even aware of! We blamed each other for all manner of different things.

I have to say it took me by surprise and it was only with hindsight that I realised it was my WAKE-UP call – at the time it just felt like hell!

I was physically, emotionally, mentally and spiritually overdrawn. I had nothing left to give. I woke up one morning and burst into tears whilst making the children's lunchboxes saying, so quietly that my husband had to ask me to repeat it, "I can't do this anymore".

What happened then and for a number of years afterwards, is a bit of a blur. I was on autopilot, never really giving myself real time to heal and reflect. After all, I had 2 young children to care for, a demanding full time job to keep, bills to pay including a newly acquired mortgage, plus a mountain of debt. I was behaving like superwoman (although I read somewhere that she didn't have any children, isn't that funny?!). I never had much time for *me*; I was too busy keeping life together.

I did, briefly, see a counsellor just before the separation, which was so powerful that it was to set me on the next step of my journey.

Wake-Up Call #2

I did not seek any more help until after my second WAKE-UP call about 5 years later.

A whirlwind of a relationship came suddenly to an end, and I decided that I would move closer to my family. Within 6 months, I had decided to quit my job to go self-employed!

Hindsight is a wonderful teacher – a little more thought and a lot less reaction might have prevented a 5-year detour of my life but, then again, it would have deprived me of the amazing people I met and the insights that I gained.

It was during this detour that I started on a journey which has led me to where I am now. I had studied counselling and qualified as a coach after the first WAKE-UP CALL. I then became a Master Practitioner of NLP (Neuro Linguistic Programming) and a Spiritual Practitioner. Each of these gave me insight into who I was and how much my past was not only affecting my present but also shaping my future. It became clear that the breakup with my husband had nothing to do with him personally, but was all about my own doubts, fears and needs. None of which I had been aware of.

Wake-Up Call #3

I have learned that life and the universe has a habit of throwing you BIG messages when you are not listening, so my soul gave me my 3rd WAKE-UP CALL! I was given notice by my landlord; I was once again in serious debt; my business was not yet performing well enough to pay 3 people. I was not earning enough to pay a living salary, so I had to get a job, quick.

It was the combination of this, plus the breakup of another relationship and a viral infection which floored me for several weeks, that made me sit up and think. Life was not going well.

- ❖ What the hell was going on?
- ❖ How could I be doing this all again?

❖ Why did I feel so ill?

However, being poorly gave me the time and space for the self-reflection that I needed in order to realise that there was a pattern going on; the one thing that was common in all these events was ME!

What on earth was I doing wrong?

Just asking that question and being ready to give up was all that was required for me to sit up. Life and the universe has a very healthy way of getting you back on the right track. I found a flat that was perfect for me and my teenage daughter, I was offered a job after the first interview I went to and I now had a way of clearing my debt mountain – Life was picking up!

One of the things that made the biggest difference was being able to pay for and see my good friend and Cognitive Hypnotherapist, Carole Samuda, for about 18 months, working through my issues and how on earth was I creating such turmoil in my life, before finally having an 'ah-ha' moment! At least enough of one to allow me to move forward!

I ended up training as a Cognitive Hypnotherapist myself with Trevor Sylvester of The Quest Institute, a man whose approach I found inspiring. I learned so much more about myself, building on the lessons that the Counselling, Coaching and NLP had provided. (I also trained as a Spiritual Practitioner).

This book is written for those people who, like me, have forgotten who they really are; who play too many roles; who do not realise how disconnected they are from themselves and have lost their way; for those people who are discovering that what is wrong is not *'out there'*, but more *'in here'* (mind, body, heart and soul).

Whilst many people believe it is their external experiences that they are dissatisfied with, I have learnt that actually it is what is actually going on inside that matters, which I explain more in the Perceptions section. I shall take you on a journey of exploration to identify the <u>real</u> root of your problems which started with that early conditioning, which set your beliefs, (1st Key) about what is important to you (Values) and the important role that your emotions (2nd Key) play which influence your thoughts (3rd Key) and then result in the creation of you habits and behavior (4th Key) that shape your choices/decisions that create your Model of the World (or your experiences and the 5th Key) that is yours alone.

I will explain in this book:

❖ How your life has not really been your own, until now.

❖ How you have been conditioned to feel and think and act in a certain way from an early age, which has directly impacted your life.

❖ How you have learned to respond to triggers in your world over which you have no control.

❖ How you can take back control, to become more empowered, more confident, happier, healthier, wealthier and maybe just wiser!

❖ How to rediscover your drive and reclaim your happiness

By exploring these hidden depths, you can begin to understand the keys that will unlock your life and the future that you have always wanted.

If this makes sense to you, please read on.

SECTION SUMMARY

In this section, you have learnt:

❖ When you begin to question who you are, what you are doing and where you are going, it is time for change – your Wake-UP Call for life

❖ Your Wake-Up call is your chance to build the life YOU really want

❖ If you do not listen to this Wake-UP call, it will continue to come knocking, only getting bigger and louder until you will be unable to ignore it any longer.

❖ That the issue is not 'out there' in the world, but 'in here' in our inner world, our heart, our mind, our body and where appropriate our spirituality

❖ You (and everyone else on this planet) has created your own unique idea of what the world is like, called a 'Model of the World'

CHAPTER 2
MIDLIFE IS NOT A CRISIS

It's a 'Wake-Up' Call?

I have seen many people over the years who have experienced a difficulty in an area of life and, as a result, have made radical changes like I did, only to find that they were no better off or that there were issues popping up elsewhere. The grass was not so green on the other side. Like them, I had not appreciated when I was younger how much our external world is just a symptom of what is going on internally.

This book is all about explaining that internal world and providing some exercises to help you identify, clear and let go, release and to change those things that no longer work for you! That you can set new parameters that will support you in the future.

Because You Can!

Everything you have ever learned about your world started when you were a baby, (I believe in the womb) through childhood and as a young adult, building the foundation of your world from your own experiences; learning from

- ❖ Your parents
- ❖ Your family
- ❖ Friends
- ❖ People in authority
- ❖ May be religion
- ❖ Your society in which you were raised.
- ❖ Workplace
- ❖ School and other learning institutions

You were conditioned into certain ways of thinking, ways that even now you may not realise are not completely your own. For example, believing that "money is scarce" or "you have to work hard for a living". As you have travelled this journey called life, you have reinforced those beliefs through the decisions you haven taken. This in turn ends up reinforcing your perception, because that is what your senses are now tuned to pick up, until over time, you have moved further and further away from who you really are. Each experience, each person you interact with and each decision you take is based on your past that were initially learned from childhood. Each step, potentially taking you further and further in the wrong direction. You know what I mean...

- ❖ Times when you really wanted to go travelling, but somehow someone or something got in the way.
- ❖ You really wanted a certain job, but there was another expectation of what you should be doing or you were told you couldn't do it.

❖ You had a dream, but life took you in another direction.

❖ You were going to change the world, but actually the only thing that really changed was YOU.

Then something happens and you WAKE-UP and you wonder:

❖ Is this it?

❖ What happened?

❖ Where has the time gone?

❖ What is the point?

❖ Who am I?

❖ How did I get here?

❖ I am done!

This is your soul, your inner voice, your Unconscious, a deeper part of you crying out to be heard. It is just that sometimes even the most difficult of situations, feels safe, so that have to get so painful, to make you sit up and take notice.

Why Ignoring Doesn't Work

The trouble with most people (me included) is that they do not change anything until it becomes so uncomfortable, painful or disagreeable that there is no option. They are forced to face up to reality. People are motivated by pleasure and mostly, if not actively, to avoid the nasty stuff, so when things are not going well, they tend to be unaware that these difficulties could contain messages for them. The trouble is that your soul will continue to make life more difficult in a number of ways (you will note mine was job, relationship and money) until you have no alternative but to take some sort of action. If you look to make changes in your outer world, based on what you are experiencing, that will resolve it right? No, it won't, because that is just the symptom. The true message needs to be understood first otherwise the action you take will be based on your previously learnt experience, your past, so that you can find yourself just repeating the same mistakes you have in the past. What is that saying "If you always do what you have always done, you will always get what you have always got"? So, it may not be what is truly right for this you, you could be right now and your future.

Your External World is a Mirror of Your Internal World

Once you begin to understand, right now, you are a sum of all your past conditioning, experiences and beliefs, it makes sense that to avoid making the same mistakes, it is necessary to explore what is no longer working for you. Then you can begin to ensure that you are making better and stronger decisions or choices, more empowering and deeper lasting changes.

So how do you become aware of what is going on internally for you with those key elements of beliefs, values, emotions, habits/behaviours, how do you identify the experiences externally, which collectively make up you and understand what they are telling you? How do each of these elements contribute to the results you are seeing in your world.

People tend to notice things more easily in their external world, so that is a good place to start. Let me share a story with you.

The Job Interview

There were two candidates called in for a job interview. The first candidate arrived at reception promptly and after explaining why they were there, asked the receptionist what the people were like in the company.

The receptionist answered:" What are they like where you work now?"

"Ah!" Exclaimed the candidate. "They are very difficult people, always moaning and complaining, and I will be glad to get out of there!"

"Well," said the receptionist, "I think you will find the people here like that too".

When the second candidate arrived, and checked in, they also asked what the people were like in the company. Again, the receptionist asked: "What are they like where you work now?" The second candidate paused, a smile forming on their face, "They are lovely people, always willing to help out and support each other and I will miss them".

"Well," said the receptionist, "I think you will find that the here are like that too".

What Does This Mean for You?

If you believe or have an expectation about your world, your brain will do everything to ensure that this is what you experience (it doesn't like to be wrong, as it operates on 'what it knows' as a way of keeping you safe). So, if you believe that your job is rubbish and that people are rude or disrespectful, the question is what could this say about you? What is it that you have learnt or believe about yourself and your world that makes this true? This is not a judgement question, it is a question to point out that maybe there is something to look at internally that is may need to be healed or changed within you. Because how can you criticise yourself for something you didn't know? Would you do that to a loved one, your child or good friend? The answer is *no*, (or at least I would hope so) and you deserve to treat yourself well too! You are the most important person in your world. How do I know? Because the people in your life are not you, only you can be you. If you have discovered something that you do not like about yourself, this in itself suggests that there is something within you which needs to change.

Tough questions, I know, but, this is the first step to lead you to something at a much deeper level which has created your world in a certain way.

In this book, I will explain in more detail, the 5 keys that will help you to get closer to this real you and how your brain filters your world before you are even consciously aware of it:

1. Your beliefs & values
2. Your emotions
3. Your thinking
4. Your habit/behaviours
5. Results

Your Soul Calling

I believe everyone has at least 4 bodies; physical, mental, emotional and spiritual.

At any point in time, each key or level will have been communicating in their own way with you. However, you were unlikely to have recognized these messages, as you have not been taught to hear them, interpret them or even to realise that this is your own inner wisdom whispering to you. You are constantly being sent clues and messages, and now is the time to learn the language of your soul. Modern life has taken us away from who we are, we have stopped listening and understanding the most powerful thing in the universe – ourselves. However, now your external world has caused you an issue big enough *that you have WOKEN UP*. Perhaps you have:

❖ realised life has been passing you by;

❖ ended up in a relationship or job that is no longer fulfilling;

❖ a feeling of being low, depressed, restless, unhappy, numb and don't know what to do about it;

❖ a nagging feeling something is not right, but you can't work out what it is;

❖ recently experienced (or are experiencing) a major life event which has sent everything you know into a tailspin (i.e. divorce, bereavement, illness, redundancy);

❖ a milestone birthday that just gets you thinking about where you are in life;

❖ a reoccurring life pattern such as debt, minor accidents, disagreements or dissatisfaction with life, problem relationships etc.

This is it! This is your soul shouting at you! Does any of this feel right? Sound familiar? Or just make sense? Yes? Then this book is for you! It is time... YOUR TIME.

All Is As It Should Be

Before I go any further, there are couple of things I would like you to understand.

❖ You are okay – you are exactly where you need to be right now.

❖ You may feel separated, misunderstood and alone at this time, but this state is necessary in order for to blossom, like a butterfly into the real you.

❖ This process needs to be judgement free, not a reason to admonish yourself, feel angry, fearful or guilty about it. Awareness creates the opportunity for change.

Many people may live their whole lives asleep regarding their own potential, but you are different. You are reading this book; you are ready for a different way – your soul has been calling and you have heard it. But just like a radio station which is not quite tuned in, the messages are unclear. As you work your way through this book I will share with you how to bust through the interference - to help you get to the core of who you are - to BE MORE YOU!

Now is just the right time for you to listen to what you already know deep inside yourself. What is it that you have forgotten? What is it that you have learnt in the past that has led you to where you are now? Now you can find out and know all is as it should be.

Health Warning!

This does all come with a health warning. Naturally, a Midlife event is a time that many people make BIG decisions without really understanding what is going on for them. They believe that if they make the changes, then love, success and happiness will come and, of course, it may, for some people.

But before you start deciding that things are not right and throwing caution to the wind, be careful! Pause Review and Reflect. Stay in your job, relationship and home, until you have worked out what you really want.

For many, perhaps this could mean being clear about what you really want from life; understanding what happiness truly means for you, not what you have been conditioned to believe it is; what is important to you about your life and the people in it; noticing the emotional and thought patterns that are supporting you and those that are not; recognizing the habits and behaviours that you are displaying; observing the experiences you are getting in all areas of life. From this you will be identifying what inner work needs to be done first. For many this may be a love that is right for you, happiness and fulfilment; feeling of safety and security, confidence and worthiness; Success and recognition, whatever it maybe for you, let's start this journey of self-discovery to find out who you really are, what you really want and how you can get there.

Are you ready? Then let's begin!

SECTION SUMMARY

In this section, you are have learnt:

- ❖ How you are conditioned from birth to be who you are today
- ❖ Beginning to understand your Wake-Up call
- ❖ That your external world is a reflection of your internal world of emotions, thoughts, responses and memories
- ❖ How to use your external world as a guide to what needs to be addressed
- ❖ Your mind has learnt a series of 'rules' and memories, that means it filters your world to those things that agree with it, discarding anything else.
- ❖ The 5 keys to getting closer to the real you
- ❖ There are 4 bodies that are essential to

create balance for a happier life

❖ That your soul communicates with you in many different ways

❖ Everything that has happened to you up until now is OK, it is what you do now and for your future that matters

❖ Before making BIG change, understand yourself first, so that in your future, you are more important in your world than ever before

CHAPTER 3
PERCEPTIONS

How Did You Get Here?

When you were conceived, you were like a blank sheet of paper. There were no stories, no beliefs, no emotions, no thoughts or experiences of the world.

It is believed that at about 8 weeks' gestation a feotus begins to 'feel' things, as the nervous system is developing. Taste and smell begins to develop at about 14 weeks, whilst the baby's ability to recognize the sound of mum starts around 16 weeks, only becoming fully developed after 24 weeks. At around 32 weeks the baby is becoming sensitive to light as they begin to track the cycle of day and night. I tell you this, because you can start to see that from as early as the womb, a baby is beginning to experience and learn it's world through that of its mother.

By the time you are born, you have already started to create your experience of the world. Only now it will begin to develop rapidly, as the experience is direct now.

You can now use your five senses to start taking in everything that is going on around you with all of that information being sent to the brain, whose primary function is to keep you safe. To do this your brain needs to understand what is good and what is not, what is safe and what is not. So, it starts processing all information accordingly and storing it away for future use. This is important to understand as it is directly responsible for the you now. It is essential that the brain learns to respond to 'known' situations in order for it to have more space and time to watch and protect. As such, it begins to learn patterns, habits and beliefs that help it process all information it receives more effectively and quickly. Let me explain – how do you know a door is a door?

You "know" what a door is, in all of its many forms, from plastic to metal, from functional to designer, size, shape etc. and you probably learned this from your parents, your teachers and books. But when you first came across a door, you needed to learn what it was, how it can actually hurt you (if your fingers are in the way and it closes for example), how to use it and its different purposes. The brain passes this information back into the memory ready to be accessed whenever you come across another door, in the future. Each time you do, any differences are added to that memory bank so that you get more and more of a sense of what the different variants of a door are like.

What this means is that when you see a door, your brain does not have to re-learn what it is and what you do with it. It just knows and in a fraction of a second, so do you. It has gone into your memory bank of files held in the part of the brain known as the Unconscious (or subconscious) mind, searched for that information and presented it to you, without you even knowing, consciously that the process has happened!

All of your experiences will have been processed in the same way. Some will be good, some will be bad, some will be safe and some will be dangerous. Some will be fun and some will be scary and so on.

Each time you have an experience the body will produce a bio electrical and chemical reaction at the same time, instructing the body as to what it needs to do. One set of these reactions is known as emotions and for extreme experiences, (usually the ones you remember) there will be an emotional (bio-chemical) and mental (electrical - chemical) memory attached to it. I believe that these responses are stored within all the cells of our body and this is important for the work that I do. Fortunately, science is beginning to prove it too. (Bruce Lipton, The Biology of Belief) As a result, everything you have experienced since being in the womb has been processed, analysed, attached to an emotional response and being filed away by the brain as to whether it is good for you or not.

As a young child who knew very little, you were reliant on others to teach you what you needed to learn. So, if your learning came from your parents, school, friends, teachers, work, doctors, society, religion, country etc., you could you now begin to see that they were also taught by people in their world, using the same process themselves since they were babies. If so, what does this mean? It means, that potentially, what they are teaching you and instilling within you, are their own learned beliefs, their values and behaviours, that are probably not really their own either, but just an accumulation from our forebears that enables patterns of beliefs and behaviours to be passed from one generation to the next.

This information is stored deep in your memory banks and cellular structure (library if you will), and only accessible when an outside event triggers the retrieval of the information.

Your brain instantly accesses this library in a fraction of a second, whenever it needs to make choices or decisions faster, generally without your conscious mind actually knowing about it. The danger with this of course, is that you are not in as much control as you think you are. And one of the visible ways it does this is via our habits. For example, you rarely think about how you make a cup of coffee, what route to take to work, what sock you put on first, lots of small decisions being taken automatically, that you do not give a (conscious) thought to. Your brain is now acting like a filter to everything you experience and do. Habits being a repetitive behavior that you are not even aware of, enabling your mind to focus on the unknown.

By your early twenties much of this information is already hardwired and is either added to or subtracted from your memory banks according to how your life plays out. And you are completely unaware of most of that information.

So, what does this mean for the you of today? It means that you are potentially living up to 95% of your life unconsciously with your day being based around what your brain understands of the past, through your experiences. I don't know if that is true, but I do believe much of our way of being is no longer as conscious as we like to think it is.

The challenge when searching for what is or isn't working for you is that this conditioning is entirely unique to you. Even if you have siblings you will probably find that your experiences will be different to theirs. Let me explain. Have you ever been to a party with someone you are close to and when you leave, one of you has had a great time and the other thought it was rubbish? Well this is the brain's filters being used to process the same information differently. Deciding what is important to you or isn't, what to draw your attention to or what to avoid.

So, is it any wonder that throughout your life you have made choices and decisions that were less than healthy for you or just downright wrong? And this information continues to be added to all the time, even now as you are reading this.

But then you arrive at your WAKE-UP call.

The one where you are so beaten down by life, so fed up of decisions that seemed right at the time but in the end, were not, and you are stuck somewhere that feels like there is no way out. So how do you know that you are ready for change, something that is long lasting and more empowering for you? Read on to understand the 5 ways you can begin to identify what is working for you or not.

Clue 1: Questioning Yourself

WAKE-UP calls come in as many different ways as there are people and sometimes it is only afterwards that we realise how life changing something was.

Whilst Midlife can be an opportunity to re-start life, it generally involves much soul searching because what is wrong may either not be quite so evident, or the problem is clear but the solution is not.

Now that you are beginning to understand that you are a product of the environment that you grew up in, the way that society has conditioned you and the decisions and choices you have made as a result, which have led you to where you are today. Just imagine how life could be different for you if some of those old learnings could be replaced and you could become a much better version of yourself, become who you are really are.

One of the first signs that you are at a crossroads of life is when you start asking yourself bigger questions. Use Exercise 1 with your big question (who am I? What am I doing? What is not working? Etc.) to discover more about what is going on for you.

Exercise 1: Inner Search

Just in case you need some help, when completing this exercise here are some typical questions that you might ask yourself, but feel free to use your own.

- ❖ Is this it?
- ❖ What happened?
- ❖ Where has the time gone?
- ❖ What is the point?
- ❖ How did I get here?
- ❖ Who am I?
- ❖ What am I doing?
- ❖ Where am I?
- ❖ What does my future hold?

You will need to get yourself a pen and a few sheets of A4 paper.

The aim of the exercise is to keep writing, no matter what, for 5 minutes without taking your pen off the page. Just write whatever comes into your head, without filtering (I can't write that, that is bad, I don't want people to know). You can destroy (burn carefully or shred) the paper afterwards. No one except you needs to see it.

You may find that the words dry up and this is completely normal. When this happens, continue to write the last word repeatedly or anything that you now find comes up in your mind (your name, I am not sure why I doing this, this is pointless, la, la, la) anything at all, just keep writing something until the thoughts flow again (and they will) and carry on until the 5 minutes is up, remembering to keep the pen moving on the paper!

This is an excellent exercise to "get out of your own way". I learned this technique when studying counselling and I still do it myself from time to time.

What happens here is that your Conscious mind starts the process and once that dries up it allows space (the repeat writing) for the deeper part of the mind to search for the answers to the questions. The funny thing about the brain is that it doesn't like an unanswered question, so once you have set it a task it needs to deliver.

Once you are done, stop and pause. Reflect on what you have written. What did you discover? Was it everything you already knew or did you get a new perspective on an old problem? Maybe something completely new came out, that has left you thinking.

For some people just the act of writing makes them feel better – did that work for you? Does it feel easier or better? Sometimes people can feel worse, but this is just the emotion moving through the body (see the section on emotions to find out what you can do to help the process).

Sometimes the stuff in your head just goes around and round and you never really address it. However, once it is out on paper it can take on a different energy which can often provide some sort of relief. In my experience, over-thinkers (see later in the book under Thinking) tend to hold everything in their head. By downloading it onto paper (a pre-historic form of computer) it is possible to create space that can result in feeling calmer. (Remember the brain likes space to enable it to protect you).

I mentioned earlier about destroying the paper, particularly if it has raised memories or emotions that are too difficult. Burning or shredding (usual health and safety stuff applies here), is a metaphor for letting go or releasing it to the Universe. You might be surprised how just doing that can help. Up until now it has been trapped inside your head (or your body) but now something has shifted, been released, taken out, shaken down and viewed from a different perspective.

There! Change is already starting to happen at that deeper level – but there is so much more you could do, so carry on reading.

Clue 2: The Signs

The signs have always been there, just not in a way that you have been taught to recognize or listen to. Feelings, patterns (time, responses from people, words etc.), reoccurring thoughts or experiences, habits, colours, music, smells, tastes, repeated phrases or words that you use, activities, people or environments that inspire or drain you, little accidents or clumsiness, colds and flu, a plethora of ways that let you know where you are at any one time in life.

This is your internal wisdom, your soul whispering to you, although you didn't know it or you have ignored it, perhaps even thought 'that's who I am'.

However, you are now learning that your soul is very persistent and will keep raising the stakes, making things louder and more difficult for you until you take notice.

The first thing to be aware of, is how your world is making you feel, maybe angry, sad, fearful or depressed. Notice those things you don't like, those things that cause you difficulty or unhappiness. This is powerful for you as you can now begin to ask the right questions and challenge yourself more, maybe using the earlier exercise of automatic writing. Alternatively, you could just capture these over a period of time say a few weeks. Nothing to do at this time, just note them and be aware of them. Awareness may just be enough to change behavior and if not, the exercises later in this book will help.

Now you are beginning to discover more about who you really are and what has got you to this point. You are beginning to listen.

Clue 3: Language

Do you ever find yourself making excuses or proffering reasons why you haven't done something? Except they are the same old excuses, same old reasons. This is just one clue as to a belief filter in operation. Other words or phrases that let you know something is not working for you, they include:

- ❖ Because
- ❖ I can't
- ❖ I have to
- ❖ I must
- ❖ I should
- ❖ I could

Kim Searle

- ❖ No time
- ❖ I will try
- ❖ But
- ❖ I always
- ❖ I need

All of these are phrases that everyone naturally uses at one time or another, but what if it is your go to phrase that you use all the time with others, or worse, about or for yourself? Are you aware of them?

Alternatively, how about the language you use regularly, 'I am p*ssed off...", "I hate...", "I am sick and tired" "I can't beat this", "I am always late", "there is never enough time", "I am fed up" etc. Repeating phrases or words like this often, drives it into the Unconscious. (remember that repetition makes something a habit) This is because Unconscious relies on the information from our senses so cannot recognized the difference between real and not real, true or not true, or positive or negative. (Have you ever said to a child 'don't do something' and they promptly did? They are not doing it deliberately; the brain just does not understand the word don't at that age!). The Unconscious then, works purely in the moment, relying on the information coming from the filters (senses – see section Conscious vs Unconscious Minds) and takes its lead from how you feel and what you think in the moment and compares to the past to result in behavior, habit and action.

"I have to....get this work done/do the washing/be on time". Yes, there are times when you HAVE, MUST, SHOULD, OUGHT but according to whom? And once you have that clear, does it mean every time? Really? How is that working for you? What do YOU want?

Perhaps now it is time to challenge them? Do you 'HAVE to go to Aunty Jean's every Wednesday afternoon'? The 'HAVE to's come from someone's expectation of you, but not from a place of wanting to, so not a good energy for you or Aunty Jean.

Is it what is expected of you by family, friends, society etc.? Is it an expectation that you have placed on yourself based on some outdated belief? Maybe you are doing it because there is no-one else? I am not suggesting you stop going to Aunty Jean's every Wednesday. What I am saying is that anything you are doing with those words listed above, is not coming from the right energy (desire or want) for you or Aunty Jean. It is time to review what is going on and if going to Aunty Jean's is important to you, then changing the language around it will be very powerful in making it more enjoyable for you both! Ask yourself these sorts of questions:

- ❖ What would happen if you didn't go every Wednesday?
- ❖ What wouldn't happen if you didn't go every Wednesday?
- ❖ What would happen if you continued to go every Wednesday?
- ❖ What wouldn't happen if you continued to go every Wednesday?

Just asking these types of questions, can begin to shake things loose in your mind, so that you can be more objective about what you are doing. Changing the HAVE to, perhaps to a want to or changing how you feel about what you are doing. Remember it is about being more aware of what is going on for you.

What if instead of "I can't" you said "I can"? Instead of "I must", you said "I choose to".

To be clear, this is not about positive thinking over negative thinking and it most certainly not black and white, right or wrong, good or bad. It is about a non-judgmental process of challenging yourself about what you say and do, to make sure it is working for you. It is another source of information that enables you to make an assessment as to whether you like what is going on in your life or not. You most certainly may find that going to Aunty Jean's every Wednesday afternoon doesn't work for you. If so, then that opens up a conversation with yourself about why you feel you need to doing what you are doing and even better to choose a different course of action that works for you!

What I am suggesting is that you start challenging your thoughts, the language that you use, "is that true?" If it is not, then there is definitely a deeper belief at play.

As I mentioned earlier, the beliefs, when you learnt them, were absolutely right for your younger self at the time. But life and you have both moved on.

In this ever-changing world, some of those

beliefs will be working against you, tripping you up and if you are not aware of them, you need to find them!

Clue 4: The BIG Wake-Up Call

For some people, it might be a major life event or just an insidious creeping feeling that just won't go away.

At first you may ignore it or just carry on doing what you have always done, just getting on with it, thinking that you have no choice or it is what you deserve. Perhaps you even fear the consequences if you disturb the status quo (this was me) until eventually (because you no longer have a choice) your inner wisdom/soul makes the situation unbearable and you have to do something different.

Do any of the following apply to you?

* ❖ Persistent unwanted feelings such as depression, drudgery, anxiety, boredom, irritability, numbness, dissatisfaction with everything, stuck, lost, alone, or lonely.

* ❖ A traumatic/life changing event such as bereavement, divorce/relationship breakup, ill health, redundancy or moving when you don't want to.

* ❖ Sudden desire to make radical changes in life/doing something different.

* ❖ No longer recognising the you in the mirror.

* ❖ Noticing that something is missing or confusing.

❖ Feeling trapped or tied down by responsibilities.

❖ Spending more time looking at the past rather than the future.

❖ Sudden desire to search for meaning in your life.

❖ No longer satisfied with the things you used to enjoy.

❖ Being stressed and constantly being at everyone's beck and call.

❖ Empty nest syndrome because the children are leaving/ have left home.

❖ Time of life changes such as menopause (or the male version- andropause!).

❖ Looking after aging parents.

❖ Living according to someone else's expectations (societal, educational, peers or family).

❖ Feeling life is not your own, stuck in a rut

The list is actually endless as everyone is unique and everyone has different triggers. Whilst I have focused on Midlife, I know people who have experienced these events much younger, in their 20's and 30's.

That is the reality of this process – it can happen at any time of life and to anyone. Some people may never experience such a WAKE-UP CALL, but to be honest, I am not sure they are any better off.

Generally, it has been called Midlife because this is when most people will experience similar sets of changes. As people get older the children are growing up or leaving home, there may be parents who need caring for, they have more time on their hands and possibly more money. Work may have become unsatisfying, routine or just boring. Up until that point people have been focused on achievement (home, status, family, material possessions). I read somewhere that the 20s are all about career, the 30s are all about family and the 40s are about purpose, which sums it up beautifully. Life in the 21st Century is changing -FAST – and so are our expectations. People are living longer and consequently, so are our expectations of what is still possible in our mid-life and beyond.

This second exercise is to assess where you are now. Find yourself some time to review where you are, right now, by undertaking this Life Audit.

Exercise 2: Life Audit

Below is a table to record where you are right now. I have put in a few examples of life area with a rating of 1 (very dissatisfied, not working for you) to 10 (very satisfied, working for you).

Under the 'Reasons for the Rating' column, write what made you rate it the way you did. Perhaps you gave self-care a 4 as you have no time for yourself or you rarely get the chance to get your hair done or go to the gym.

This information will be used later in the book.

Exercise 2: Life Audit Table

Life Area	Rating 1 (very dissatisfied) 10 (very satisfied)	Reason for the rating
Self-Care	*2*	*I am overweight and don't exercise. I come last on my list.*
Family	*8*	*I have a close and supportive family.*
Love		
Health & Exercise		
Finances		
Vocation/Work		

Life Area	Rating 1 (very dissatisfied) 10 (very satisfied)	Reason for the rating
Social/Fun		
Spiritual		
Contribution or Giving back		
Learning, Education or Broadening Horizons		
Other		

SECTION SUMMARY

In this section, you have learnt:

❖ More about how you begin to experience your world since before birth

❖ Your 5 senses supply the unconscious

part of your brain with information

❖ This information is processed, analysed and attached to an emotional response, filed away for future reference

❖ Messages are sent around the body bio-chemically and through electrical impulses

❖ Your unconscious mind processes information, seconds before your conscious mind does

❖ You live life up to 95% of your life unconsciously

❖ Choices and decisions you make are based on your past

❖ FIve ways to identify what is or is not working for you.

CHAPTER 4
EXPLORATION

Understanding the Brain

Did you know that science is now beginning to recognise that we have more than one brain? (Check out Dr Joe Dispenza – see Appendix 2)

For the purposes of this book, though, I will keep it simple and refer only to:

❖ the Conscious mind (that part of you that is fully aware of what is happening for you in this moment, using each of your senses); and

❖ the Unconscious mind, (that part of you that is on constant alert to make sure that you are kept safe, which includes all your bodily functions such as blinking, heart beating, blood circulating, digesting, reproducing all without you having to do a thing. Amazing, isn't it? It is also where all your memories, emotions, values, beliefs and information are stored).

The purpose of this book is to use the Conscious mind to help explore the Unconscious one. To identify what is working for you and what is not. This will then enable you to make changes that will make life happier, healthier, wealthier and better!

Unconscious vs Conscious minds

Earlier, when talking about the clues your world is giving you, I explained how you can learn when something is not working for you.

As you are reading this book, you will be aware of things around you. Maybe you are drinking coffee or sitting somewhere public and hearing the chatter and noise around you, or you may be on a beach feeling the breeze coming off the sea.

However, there is so much going on around you at any one time, even when you are at home, that if I were to ask you to close your eyes for a moment and just pay attention to ALL that you can hear, you would suddenly realise how much you were unaware of. Listen for the sounds that you hadn't heard, (the clock ticking, the central heating clicking, the birds singing outside or perhaps traffic flowing by); feel the temperature of where you are, (is there a draft or warm current of air? Pay attention to your heart beating, may be the feel of a chair you are sitting in, your feet on the floor)

If I were to ask you the name of your first pet or the colour of your front door, you could do this (in most cases) quickly. This information was not in your Conscious mind, until the question was asked. Then your UNCONSCIOUS mind in a fraction of a second, was able to pull on that information from you're your memory. So, what is the difference?

Firstly, the conscious and unconscious mind are a simpler description of the structure of your brain. The Conscious mind is focused on where you are aware right now, in the present. It is aware of what you are doing; picking up on your world through your 5 (or 6 or more) senses. This information is passed through those senses (sight, hearing, touch, taste, smell and if you believe it intuition) onto the Unconscious mind which then processes it through a number of filters (for example, beliefs, values and learnings, although there are plenty of others) it has learnt over time and re-presents that back to the Conscious mind in the form of a decision, a choice, a habitual response, a behaviour, a feeling or a thought. The important thing to note here, is that this information has already been processed by the UNCONSCIOUS mind with any decisions, choices, habits, behaviours, feelings and thoughts are decided and just presented for validation by your conscious mind!

Your Conscious mind works whilst you do and sometimes is so active, that it can keep you awake! (See the 3rd key Thinking) whereas the Unconscious is working 24 x 7 whether you are asleep or awake, always watching to keep you safe from harm. Ever woke up during the night suddenly, and not sure why? Your Unconscious has picked up on something it sees as a threat. So even when you are sleeping it is working. This is important to note. For those of you experiencing, anxiety, fear, worry, stress etc., means that somewhere your unconscious has learnt something that means it is trying to keep you safe. These emotions are there to let you know something is (potentially) wrong in your world or that you have some faulty 'programming'. You may not be in the traditional physical danger of our ancestors when the unconscious mind was most listened to, but because it doesn't 'know' the difference, in the modern world of what constitutes danger, it will still respond. If you have ever heard of the phrase Fight, Flight or Freeze, this is the response that the unconscious employs to get you to react.

Very often your unconscious takes over from the conscious mind during the day.

Have you ever been driving and suddenly realised that you have not been aware of the past 3 or 4 miles, or been washing up and found yourself daydreaming about something or somewhere more pleasant so that the job was done and you weren't even really aware?

You have been operating in an UNCONSCIOUS mode, a state that people drift into and out of every day, when the brain is doing something repetitive or what it sees as boring.

I have often likened our Unconscious mind to a computer; most people have no understanding of what is happening, only the end results.

When you first buy a computer, everything works efficiently and effectively. It is only over time the computer will begin to develop certain behaviours as it is exposed to patterns of instructions, downloaded software or hardware upgrades, bugs and viruses; it will be filled with documents, films and photos of your past and gradually it will get slower and slower. This is just like your Unconscious mind, with memory, storage space, bugs and viruses at play, or applications that are out of date. And this is all stored away, out of your conscious mind, which needs to focus on the now.

So Why Is This Important?

The Unconscious information is generally unknown Consciously, unless triggered where we then just react or take action, but not without necessarily questioning what we are doing. But the Unconscious and Conscious minds are in constant communication with each other.

The Unconscious communicates not in sentences, but rather through symbols, metaphors, patterns, repeated experiences, aches, pains, illness, emotions, thoughts, imagination, sensations, dreams, inspirations always letting you how things are for you. I have identified these into 5 keys.

1st Key: Beliefs and Values

You have now been introduced to the concept of a WAKE-UP call.

❖ You are beginning to understood that you are operating a system that is not completely your own, you have been conditioned from since before birth.

❖ You have started to investigate the big questions for you and they may or may not have highlighted some surprises.

❖ By now you will have hopefully completed a Life Audit in Exercise 2.

❖ You have found some of the ways to identify what is working for you and what is not.

❖ You have now been introduced to the Conscious and Unconscious mind and why you will not have been aware of how your beliefs, values, emotions and memories could be affecting you.

Are you ready to follow these clues and do some Soul searching?

Are you willing to face even the most difficult truths if it means you can change life in a way that works for you?

Excellent!

Everyone has a set of beliefs of some kind, beliefs that they live by. "I am punctual", "I have to have coffee before I do anything" 'You have to work hard for your money', 'life is not safe' etc.

What Are Beliefs Then?

I want you to know that I completely understand that some of these beliefs may seem very real to you. According to author Andrew Matthews, "We all believe something slightly different about the world and (yet) we all know what we believe is right".

A belief is an acceptance that something exists or is true, but is not generally based on fact.

Most beliefs were learned as a child, such as not being late, clearing your plate, etc.and may have been easy to follow in your younger years, particularly as you were doing as you were told – usually by your parents or other adult! Now as an adult that belief of being on time is causing you issues as you attempt to hold down a career, sort out the children, look out for parents, walk the dog, feed the cat, have time for you partner and, if you are lucky, time for yourself! Suddenly that inner belief of being punctual is putting you under pressure and potentially causing issues as you find yourself struggling to keep up with everything.

Because you have lived with these beliefs all your life, they have become such a part of who you are that you don't even think about them, let alone question them. For some people they assume and, may expect, that these beliefs are the same for everyone starting all manner of confusion and conflict. How often are you on time and your best friend is late – does that frustrate you?

For example, if you believe (and I did) that you have to work hard for a living, to make ends meet, then you are right. Your brain does not like to be wrong and will endeavour to ensure that this rule, the belief, is maintained in your life no matter what, unless it begins to threaten your safety!

Where Did These Beliefs Come From?

Repeated Phrases

Did you ever get told or hear any of the following?

- ❖ Don't be stupid
- ❖ Big boys don't cry
- ❖ You're useless
- ❖ You're rubbish at....
- ❖ What were you thinking?
- ❖ Money doesn't grow on trees
- ❖ You have to work hard to be a success
- ❖ You don't get something for nothing
- ❖ You can't.

Unfortunately said by (and generally not to cause you harm) our parents and family and then our wider world of school, work, society, religion etc. When this happens just a few times and provided it does not cause you a big emotional reaction, then it does not automatically become a new rule/belief. However, if it is constantly repeated or when accompanied by a strong emotion, (see next section) then the unconscious mind, feeling you are under attack, learns a new rule (belief) to keep you safe.

Remember, all adults were also taught the same thing. Phrases like this do tend to run in families and it is only when challenged that these patterns can be changed for our children.

Significant Emotional Events

Another way in which it is possible to create a belief, is if there is a significant emotional event, which the unconscious mind stores with the belief. And the more senses that were involved in the creation of that memory, the stronger the influence it will have over the experiences you have later in life.

When seeing clients for phobias, there is usually one particular event that they can recall where they were shocked or scared out of what they were doing, back into the moment (children live in a different world to us most of the time up to the age of 8). This shock will have been as a result of having at least 3 senses engaged at once (visual, touch, auditory, sometimes taste and/or smell). At that moment, the unconscious mind searches for the root of the shock and finds something that seems to be the cause. (This is not always the something that was the cause either). So, the unconscious mind forms a new rule/belief that the 'perceived cause' is dangerous, and consequently each and every incident going forwards results in a reaction that becomes a behavior, then a habit and then a phobia. (it should be noted that not all such incidents become phobias, there are a plethora of other factors at play). Similarly, other incidents in childhood (and later in life such as a loss, car accident, relationship breakup, where you begin to believe you are completely alone, not safe, or you can't trust others) can result in a similar effect and be stored in the memory as a belief, and you may have no conscious recollection of it being there.

Obviously, it is more complex than this, but I think you can understand what I am suggesting here.

What is interesting to note is that people can have the same belief but live it in very different ways. There is the story of two boys of an alcoholic father. The first one stated that the reason he drank was because his Father drank, whilst the second one rarely drank and explained it was because his Father drank. Both had been exposed to the same experience, but had 'chosen', on some deeper level, to deal with it very differently. The same can happen with a belief – either it puts you in a powerless state or a driven one.

Over time these beliefs become repeated so often that, like a footpath through the woods that has been well trodden, it is easier to keep treading the same path because it is what you know (also see the Habits section) and before long you develop the behaviours that become habits, which is why you may not be aware of them! Buddha is famously quoted as saying "watch your words, they become actions; watch your actions, they become habits; watch your habits, they become character; watch your character, for it becomes your destiny."

Before you know it, if you hear these regularly enough (it is said that our beliefs are just thoughts that people think over and over again), they become who you are and you start acting them out in your life.

Peer Pressure

Very often in families, social, peer or work groups, you may find that there is an expectation of how you should be in order to fit in or be accepted, you have to learn a way of being that perhaps does not fit with who you really are and before you know it, they become part of you.

I experienced this when working as a Project Manager. A key part of the role is to identify and manage issues and risks and I did this easily. However, I soon found that I was doing this in my personal life too. People don't always want solutions, and my wanting to help by providing them, didn't always go down well. I became frustrated by people complaining about their lives (issues) and worries (risks) and not doing anything about them! I couldn't understand why!

How do Beliefs Affect Me?

The biggest issue with beliefs is that when things are not working for you, it is easy to look outside of yourself for the solution. Which makes sense right? Whilst this can work, you will not find and correct the root cause, the belief or decision that you took in the past. The chances are you might experience it again and again, albeit in different guises. Maybe you believe that your life is not going well because of the job, the boss, the banks, the government, everyone. Only you are learning a new way of being. Where if something is not working for you, you know it is a message from your unconscious mind that something deeper is going on.

The longer the belief has been around, the deeper it has been ingrained in your neural pathways and, a bit like clearing the garden of weeds, it can take some time to eradicate the belief completely on your own. There is an exercise later in the Emotions section that can help speed this process up – all you need to do for now is make a note of what is going on for you!

Beliefs can be formed at any time and eventually when reinforced regularly in their experience, people accept them as true. Everyone has them, dictating how they relate to their world. Beliefs are held deep within and you are probably not aware that they exist as they have become part of you and you don't know any differently. The worse thing is that these beliefs can hold you back from being the best you can be. (Others will be absolutely working for you, but as this book is looking to helping you, it is looking at ones that are getting in the way). They are making your world smaller and smaller. It is not who are what you are meant to be!

The question needs to be "Is this who I really am?" or "have I just been conditioned this way?"

The good news is you can change those beliefs that are not working for you! And you could find that as you clear away more and more of those old beliefs about yourself you could begin to open yourself up to more and better opportunities!

Remember that the brain is always trying to keep you safe, to move you towards pleasure and away from pain. Whilst just changing a thought process can be simple for some things or some people, for others it can be quite challenging.

Exercise 3 Identify Key Limiting Beliefs

First of all how do you identify the problem belief?

To make this simple, I have listed a set of the most common beliefs that people hold about themselves that get in their way. Take one of the areas that you identified in your life audit that you would like to work on most, and ask yourself, what do I belief about myself in relation to this?

You may find others that I have not listed or that that there is more than one that applies and this is okay – it doesn't mean you are bonkers! It just means that it was another rule you learned to protect yourself at some point. And some of them may sound quite ridiculous when you say them out loud, but deep in your heart you know they are true.

Look at the list of common limiting beliefs below and rate them with 1 – not something you believe, or 10 - you believe completely.

When doing this exercise, put the first answer that comes into your head; before logical, sensible you start to justify your answer. Do not give it much thought. By answering quickly, the first thought is likely to be your Unconscious answering before your cognitive mind (always lagging a bit behind) can interrupt with objections! Any delay will be your Conscious mind 'thinking' about the answer. Please suspend all judgement about how many you circle or any that you circle you don't understand, it is just an exercise to find out what is going on.

Exercise 3: Key Limiting Beliefs Table

Limiting Belief	Rating 1 - 10
I am not worthy	
I don't deserve it	
I am not important	
I am stupid/fat/ugly	
I am not loved/ unlovable	
I feel abandoned	
I am alone	
I am a failure	
I am scared of success	
I am useless	
I am not good enough	

Limiting Belief	Rating 1 - 10
I can't do that	
I am weak	
I am too old/young	
I don't have time	
I am sick and tired	
I don't trust myself	

Another way to identify any other belief you may have that is not listed (there are many others), is to become aware of when something has:

❖ Not worked for you the way you expected, and this seems to be a pattern

❖ Resulted in a negative emotion which happens at inappropriate times or with certain triggers i.e. traffic, certain people or events

❖ You using repeated phrases such as 'I always, I must, I should, I could, I am p*ssed off, I am sick and tired'

❖ Set off your inner critic/voice that tells you off constantly

❖ Shown you some pattern that plays out in your life that you don't understand.

Once you have identified the beliefs, now it is time to question them and here are some questions to get you going!

- ❖ What is that about – and keep repeating until you get to the belief about yourself that is limiting you in some way (usually a sentence starting "I am")
- ❖ What stops me?
- ❖ What is this event/person/place teaching me?
- ❖ What do I believe that led to .... [fill in the blank with the undesired result].

Then ask yourself - is this mine? Or someone else's? Is it True? When is your first memory of this?

Sometimes, the memory that comes to mind is not immediately obvious.

Perhaps you were told off for doing something you shouldn't have been doing (eating biscuits before dinner etc.) and believed you were bad.

A parent, teacher, someone you loved saying something unkind to you or telling you off – and you believed you were unloved.

Did you try something once, failed and decided you were stupid?

Maybe you were ridiculed for your talent and were teased, leading to feelings of keeping yourself small.

Now Ask Yourself Some More Questions

- ❖ Was it based on real experience or someone else's?
- ❖ How has the belief played out in your life?
- ❖ What would life be like in 1,5,10 years if you kept this belief?

❖ Does it show up in more than one area?
  I.e. work, family sport, hobbies, health,
  money?

❖ What would be different in your life, if
  this belief were no longer true?

❖ What would be a more empowering belief
  to hold?

❖ Is it beginning to feel painful enough to
  let go of?

This may raise some emotions for you, in
which case go straight to the emotion section!

Values

Values are the way the mind prioritises
decisions in your world, what is important to
you. It is your "why" you do the things you do,
or say. For example, if money is one of your
values, you will place much time and effort on
either earning it, saving it, or getting by with it.
For example, if family is one of your values,
then you will spend as much time as possible
with them and have no problem when they
need your help.

The thing about values, (like beliefs) is that
when you created them you, most likely, were
very young. They can change over time
depending on where you are, but generally you
do not choose them Consciously.

As such, some values may not be working for
your higher good, because they are not yours
and may actually be making life miserable for
you.

What do I mean? Well, for example, if family

is one of your highest values and you do everything you can for your family, but that is not reciprocated, you might feel downtrodden, undervalued and resentful as time goes on. But because it is important to you, you just "suck it up". This value is not working for you in the right way.

As part of becoming more aware of who you are, the next exercise will help you understand your top values which will enable you to identify those that bring you happiness or fulfilment and those that are actually draining you. (This does not mean losing the value, family is important, right? But it needs to be a positive thing for you too).

Exercise 4: Values

This exercise can be invaluable on so many levels for helping to understand what is going on in your life and why you are the way you are.

For some, this exercise will present no surprises, whilst for others it will.

Please use this exercise for any area of your life that may be causing you some difficulty or where you need to make a change such as career, relationships or a life decision.

It can help by giving you an understanding of what is important to you (your values), where you will place your focus (time, money, self) and from there you can then begin to understand more about what your drivers are and what is important to you.

Step 1

Get a piece of A4 paper and pen, or a blank document on your PC. Start by asking the question, "What is important to me about [the area of life in question]?"

Then list everything that comes to mind, keep writing until you run out of things to write. If you can only think of a few things to start with you can always come back to it. These may be around beliefs; time, money, geography, your environment, people, skills and behaviours - just everything that is important to you. For example, for a new job it maybe something like:

- ❖ Within half an hour from home
- ❖ Flexible working
- ❖ Location
- ❖ Indoors or outdoors environment
- ❖ Good Rewards i.e. financial, or other benefits
- ❖ Opportunities to learn
- ❖ Career Path
- ❖ Work with people/animals/nature

Once you have filled up at least a full A4 sheet (why not see if you can do a second page? I have seen exercises where you come up with 100 reasons! But not sure they will be helpful for this particularly exercise) you are ready for the next step.

Step 2

Now review your list and begin to narrow it down to your top 10 most important things.

The aim is to put your values in order of importance with number 1 being the most important. Once you think you have done that you can move to step 3.

	What is Important to Me
1	
2	
3	
4	
5	
6	
7	
8	
9	
10	

Step 3

To check the order of importance of your values, take the first two values on your list and ask yourself, is the first value *more* important, or *less* important than the second one. If it is *more* important, leave the value at point one. If it is *less* important than the value in the second place, reverse them.

Then using the value in the second line, again ask yourself is this value *more* important or *less* important than the value in line three. If it is more important, leave the values where they are. If it is *less* important than the value on the third line, reverse them.

Repeat until you have covered all 10 values on your list.

Before continuing, how does this now look, feel or sound to you? Tweak as necessary to get the list right. You may be surprised to find that some values you expected to be the most important are not, or vice versa. If your first two or three things at the top of the list are not what you want, then at least you know now where to focus to make changes.

You now have a measure to identify whether your life reflects your values. So, if your values for work were recognition, money and growth, does your current role or company provide this? If not, then maybe it is time for a re-think?

2nd Key: Emotions

For me, some of the most undervalued parts of our makeup are our emotions. You know what I mean. You hear regularly about mind, body and soul, but no mention of emotions.

Yet emotions are the most powerful part of who you are, the real powerhouse. They let you know where you are, providing personal signposts, guiding you during troubled times and with tasks too important to leave to intellect alone. For example, dangerous situations which would not allow for the quick responses required to keep you or someone you love safe. It is your internal 'satnav' to let you know if you have strayed from the path – YOUR path.

I think it is worth exploring what emotions

are because the better you feel, the more on track you are. The worse you feel, the more off track you are, you are not being you, perhaps tolerating something or heading in the right direction.

What Are Emotions?

Emotions are integral to our thinking and vice versa. They are closely linked to the nervous system and are a bio-chemical reaction. But where they are specifically being not yet agreed upon.

For me, I like to think that they are an energy that is contained in the cells within our body, acting as our own personal (emotional) 'satnav', letting us know where we are, and whether what we are doing is good for us or not.

You may have seen it printed as E-Motion, and in some ways that is exactly how I see them - Energy in Motion. I have found over years of working with clients that emotions are held in various places around the body, although primarily around the stomach, heart and head, funnily enough. And because your whole physical being is made up of energy, emotions are just part of that physical being.

Dr Bruce H. Lipton, PH.D, a well-known cell microbiologist, has discovered that our cells are like mini human beings in that they grow and die, need nourishment and excrete, reproduce, have memory (important to note) and move towards good stuff and away from bad.

The idea that our individual cells will move

towards good things and away from the bad is an interesting one, because this is how our unconscious keeps us safe using emotions as one way to let us know what is going on in our world.

If emotions are just energy how do they become stuck?

For the most part, emotions that are expressed or released do not cause us any issue. It is only those that are denied, ignored, filed away or held on to, that can become a problem. Each one building upon another, one at a time, that they can begin to cause an issue.

It is like stacking a pile of bricks one on top of another, each new brick raising the potential vulnerability of the structure and, at any moment, one brick can bring down the whole thing. Similarly, with emotions, we may store just a few but the more we repeat something that has emotional connections, the more the risk of it all coming crumbling down is likely to occur.

And of course, repressed, unexpressed emotions end up being stored in our body somewhere. I believe some can actually turn into physical ailments like aches and pains, or possibly something more serious. But they definitely are part of the cause for anxiety and stress which cause adrenaline and cortisol to be pumped into the body as a response to fear. The result of too much adrenaline and cortisol can lead to adrenal fatigue, high blood pressure, heart disease etc. a whole new set of problems to deal with.

Where Are Emotions Stored?

It could be anywhere! The tummy, the head and the chest are the most common areas where you 'store' emotion, but, according to TCM (traditional Chinese medicine) potentially anywhere in your energy field, and they believe that depending on where the energy is 'stuck' (unexpressed) has a meaning! It doesn't matter if you can feel it or sense it, or just get a general idea of where it is, you just know that it can still be worked upon.

Because emotions are stored in the body, unless you express them, that is exactly where they stay. Some people can express and release those emotions easily, but others who may not have learned how to process emotions, because it wasn't an acceptable thing to do, because they feel they will lose control if they express them, particularly all at once, they could end up storing them somewhere in the body. Every time a trigger occurs so does an emotion and, it is so instantaneous that our Conscious mind does not even have time to process what is going on, but the unconscious' primary directive of keeping you safe is always ready and willing to act.

Importance of Emotions

Emotions are an important part of your makeup – they have developed over human evolution, as a way to warn you if something is going on, helping you to respond to your environment, FAST.

Feelings can be instantaneous and certainly as a message system, it is much faster than your conscious mind process information, which does react, but never quite so fast. They let you know that you need to be on your guard, by creating an appropriate response. Have you ever walked into a room where an argument has taken place and you can sense the atmosphere? That! Met someone, where you have taken an instant dislike to someone and you have no idea why, just that you don't like them? That! Known something is wrong in a relationship, but can't quite work out what is going on? That.

All examples of where your unconscious is picking up on signals you are not (yet) consciously aware of. Whether you should get the hell out of wherever you are (flee) or stay stand your ground (fight) your unconscious will flood your system with adrenaline and cortisol to keep you safe. Where you experience the freeze part of this process, this just suggests some conflicting "rules" such as 2 beliefs that are incompatible or your conscious mind has got involved, so you do nothing.

They are such an important mechanism to ensure that you are kept safe and yet somehow, emotions are frowned upon. As young children, you may learn that they are not to be expressed outwardly and, for some of you like me, you may bottle them up, contain them and pretend they are not there – not good!

But emotions are an important way that your Unconscious can communicate with you.

They need to be acknowledged and the

61

messages they are providing, as this will help the bio-chemical responses to move through your system. Like all energy, they need to be expressed (moved) in some way. Energy that does not move becomes stuck and like a stagnant pool of water, can cause problems.

People tend to be afraid of emotions – your logical conscious self is suspicious of emotions, thinking they are irrational, scared of what might happen if they are in control, chaos could reign. Increasingly over a few hundred years, Western culture in particular, has advocated a more rational approach to life. What people do not appreciate is that the supposed irrational emotions are just messages and when they are expressed appropriately and addressed, they will provide more harmony in life, rather than ignoring them and allowing them to flare up in an uncontrolled way. I find it interesting that once people understand the real benefits of emotions and the logical mind, we might find more balance, not just in ourselves, but our families, work and society! Until then people learn in one way or another how to hide or deny their feelings, even from themselves, learning to bury them, sometimes very deep.

What if I Ignore My Emotions?

For some people it doesn't make one jot of difference – and that is fine.

However, stuck energy will cause issues. Here are some of the ways stuck energy could be causing your unconscious, and thereby you, a problem: -

❖ Regular little accidents such as cuts and bruises – emotions aren't working so the Unconscious uses small accidents to draw our attention to something.

❖ Some physical ailment – this may seem a little controversial to suggest, but I have already explained how I believe the effects of stuck, unexpressed emotions, and there is increasing evidence that they can cause physical symptoms. Whenever I am experiencing some physical ailment I reach for the Louise Hay book "You can Heal Yourself" before I do anything. She talks about the body communicating through ailments and, whilst it may not be true for everything, I have found it to be a useful guide. Particularly when working with clients, allowing to probe with questions around specific emotions or beliefs. For the most part, if nothing else, it triggers a conversation that either proves or disproves what a client is facing!

❖ Stress and Anxiety - For years, I used to talk about being stressed; at work, at home, money, la, la, la! Only much later, did I realise the stress was actually a mixture of fear and anxiety that I had not acknowledged. My language had made it something else that I was more readily in control of. My unconscious mind just learnt that was my world and gave me more. Which meant that I am still dealing with the after effects of those emotions now. Effects such as intolerances, weight gain, high blood pressure etc. The initial feelings of anxiety and fear became my thoughts which exacerbated my feelings, which led to the over production of adrenaline and cortisol production. I am a bit of a sloth and not great with exercise, as my experiences have taught me there is pain in them.

❖ Sudden Emotional Outbursts – these may happen rarely for most people, or for some people frequently, but you can be sure that they are masking a larger and deeper well of emotions just waiting to be acknowledged and expressed more appropriately.

❖ Depression –in my (model of the) world, is a suppression of a wealth of emotions (memories and experiences) which have been bottled away for so long that even the sufferer cannot pin point where they have come from. It is a way of keeping yourself safe, as expressing emotions may not have been okay in your family. It is also known that illnesses like this can run in the family so it is not surprising that as part of growing up, if one parent had a tendency towards depression, then the child will learn that way of being as well. Having experienced depression, myself, I need to be clear that the state is very real and that there is a spectrum from a little depressed to massively depressed. But I wonder, if depression can be a learned behaviour from your family, maybe it is possible you can just as easily unlearn it, can't you?

❖ Psychologically - There is a close connection between the mind and body and whilst the jury is out about which comes first (in my world it is definitely the emotions, as they are part of the original primal brain), bottled up emotions can affect the way you think. You are less likely to make strong positive decisions if you are running a fear emotion deep within you. It is also very important to note, that you cannot be logical and emotional at the same time, which is why it is not possible to rationally talk someone down in the middle of a meltdown. It is best to 'be' a place of safety to allow them to 'burn out' the emotion.

❖ Spiritually – For those of you into manifesting, Law of Attraction and The Secret, let me tell you it is not your thinking you have to master! It is your primary vibrational state of the emotions, that will make the difference! If you have old energies inside that are reflecting fear, guilt, anger, sadness, then the energies you are putting out into your world are not attracting the right things to you. You can tell yourself until you are blue in the face that all is well and you are attracting money, but if you believe you don't deserve it, your emotional energy will be vibrating that. How many times have you heard people talking about feeling 'lighter', 'happier', 'brighter' having released something they have been holding onto for a long time? That!

❖ Other people – will know more about you than you do, if you are holding onto old emotions. You know what I mean? Some people just ooze negativity through every pore. Have you ever met someone and taken an instant dislike to them? Yet you have no idea why, just something about them you didn't like. I am not saying it is purely emotional, because your Unconscious will have been picking up on some sort of energy vibration such as the way they walk, talk or conduct themselves, that is not good for you and your unconscious mind will have sent that feeling of dislike up for your attention, but the chances are emotions will have been a key part of that reason. Such people are often carrying lots of 'baggage' (a term used for emotional stuff) and have a resonating anger, are profoundly sad or grief stricken and are vibrating this out into their world.

❖ Language & Speech – This brings me nicely onto language. Emotions can also play themselves out via language. For me, I used to use the language of war (put your head above the parapet, deadline, let's fight this, scuppered, kill it dead) to describe things and when I realised I was quite shocked. It was reflecting an inner anger I had not realised I was carrying. How might it be affecting your language. Watch for what you say. Do you say you're "sorry" frequently, even when it is not your fault? Look for the common words you use to describe things – are they telling you something?

Some people get so stuck in their story (I have been one of them – apologies to family and friends!) that they repeat it over and over and over and over. They are not dealing with the issue, just replaying it. Once they finally address the underlying emotion, they may still tell the story but the emotional drag that was there before will have gone.

❖ Behaviours - I couldn't write about emotions without explaining how some of our behaviours stem from trapped emotions. The man who regularly gets into fights; the drunk who becomes morose: The person who displays a 'depressive' state; The person who cries a lot, (not just at the sad movies!); The person who slams and bangs things around; The person who doesn't spend money (or maybe overspends); Someone who over exercises or not at all; The ones who smoke, drink, take drugs, shops, or eat to handle their world? Just some of the indicators of an unexpressed emotion. What behaviours do you display that might suggest something is going on?

❖ Your Current State – can easily be affected by those pesky emotions you have stored up. Your current state reflects where you are right now, in the present moment. The thing about emotions is that they can be triggered by something seemingly innocuous such as a word, phrase, person, smell, sound or even another feeling. Which means your current state is vulnerable to a sudden change when one of these (usually) external triggers is used and then you end up responding in a way you would have preferred not to have. Triggers are a great way that your emotional 'satnav' is shouting at you! Would recognizing them be of value to you?

❖ Temperament - what is meant by this? Your temperament is how you are generally living your life and tends to be who you have become as a way of controlling your world to feel safe.

Are you generally a happy go lucky person, positive and friendly? Or a quiet introverted, thoughtful soul? Alternatively, a fearful, protective, worried soul, or an angry, "the world is out to get me" kind of soul? There is no right or wrong, you have only yourself to be honest with. This is not a judgement remember, it is simply who you have become, who you have been conditioned or programmed to be. They are just the messages to let you know you may not be who you really are.

At their core, everyone wants the same as everybody else; love, happiness, health, wealth, family etc. But the perceived happy-go-lucky person could be storing up just as much emotional baggage as the angry one, they have simply learned to deal with things differently, perhaps storing it away or ignoring it.

Of course, if you are reading this and you are happy with your emotional health then that is a great place to be and you could use this task to gain some insights into how others may be affected.

What Is My Emotion Telling Me?

I used to believe in positive and negative emotions. Being more than happy to express the positive ones and keep the negative ones for when I was alone, or just suppressing them.

What if there were no positive or negative emotions? What if that is just the judgement that you give them? I have already mentioned that I see emotions as just your 'satnav' giving you feedback on whether you are on the right path; needing to look at something that is not working for you or some old wound that has not healed and is holding you back.

According to Shakti Gawain, even positive feelings can be something to be feared. Too much happiness, love or passion can be overwhelming for some people. Have you ever experienced a person who is 'over the top' happy, in love, or constantly on a life high? It becomes tiring for those around them, as well as those individuals, whose life is not always like that. People aspire to be like celebrity, with money, fame and fortune, but we have no knowledge of how hard they have to work to keep there, whilst it puts undue pressure on people to attempt to be something they are not. Perhaps you know someone with a larger than life presence whose energy is just so overbearingly 'positive' that it just irritates you.

There is no right or wrong to understanding what your emotion is telling you, because only you will know if it is right or not. Sometimes the Unconscious will use the same memory or the same emotion to bring your attention to something because it is important, not because you didn't release it before, but it is a way of getting your attention!

Do not be surprised if you revisit some events you thought you had dealt with, as they may be appearing to provide a different perspective, and each time you can let more emotion go. It is very much trial and error and doing it on your own can be a little laborious and time intensive. However, this book is to help you speed up the process, and I have an effective tool towards the end of this section that will help.

What are the Benefits of Working with Emotions?

The ideal solution is that the head and the heart (read emotions) are aligned in their way of being as this will facilitate better choices, better decisions and therefore better output. I often see people who feel stuck, torn or conflicted. What is going on, is just an indication of faulty thinking or the head and heart working against each other. Working on an emotion to clear it, doesn't mean you will never experience that emotion again, remember they are the 'satnav' that is there to keep you informed of things you cannot Consciously be aware of (see the section on Conscious and Unconscious information). What it does mean, is that your emotional state will be more settled with fewer peaks and troughs, as you develop a better way of reacting to and coping with all the myriad of things life throws at you.

Once you have worked through those emotions that are no longer working for you, you could then begin to find you are:

* ❖ Feeling lighter.
* ❖ Freer.
* ❖ Being treating differently, by people even though it appears to you that nothing has changed.
* ❖ Making better choices and decisions for you.
* ❖ Finding that the changes are long lasting (only noticed with hindsight).
* ❖ Changing with no effort, as the work was done at the root level, in your Unconscious zone of the brain and physiology.

How Do I Let Go of the Emotion?

Everyone experiences their emotions differently and although common names are used, they vary from person to person. It is interesting to note that an emotion, say fear, can actually have an infinitesimal spectrum, from hardly any fear at one end of the spectrum, right up to extreme fear or that one person's fear is another adrenaline rush. This is important to note, as emotional descriptions are subjective and may not actually reflect the reality of what is going on for someone inside.

It is said there are really only two real emotions; love and fear and that everything else in between is a spectrum.

I have already mentioned that there seems to be a fear of 'negative' emotions, particularly the extreme ones. The Conscious, logical self is suspicious of emotions, as it can mean things getting out of control (have you ever tried to control an extreme emotion?). Certainly, in western culture there is a more rational approach to life, where emotions do not play a big part. Therefore, people very often communicate in a thinking way not a feeling way, unless they are more in touch with their heart, enabling them to communicate feelings.

We are not taught how to handle strong emotions such as fear, anger, sadness, grief or jealousy and all variants in between. Have you ever been in a position either having lost someone, or know someone who has – what do you say? What do you do for the best? We just don't have a clue. As a result, we think it is better to learn how to hide or deny feelings, even from ourselves and others. 'I'm OK' a typical response from someone who may, very clearly NOT be ok!

People can bury emotions, sometimes so deeply, they can cut themselves off from feeling at all. It doesn't mean that the emotions are not there, just that the logical mind has tuned them out, boxed them away, ignored them, or as a famous Vulcan is known to say 'illogical'. (sorry Star Trek reference, bit of a fan). But only a very small percentage of the population do not experience any emotion at all, and those that do, potentially fall into the category of requiring some sort of medical intervention.

Working with emotions may not always be an easy thing to do, because it means that:

❖ You are finally acknowledging a part of yourself that you have denied for longer than you care to mention.

❖ You have no idea what is going on.

Being able to understand or label what the emotion is (let's be honest, everyone likes a label!) can sometimes just be too difficult

Once you have found it, what do you do with it? As it can bring up other emotions!

Your ability to translate your world through your emotional responses may take some practice, because for some this is incredibly easy. For many others, particularly those who tend to live in their heads (like me), it can take a while.

To be clear, by exploring emotions does not mean that you will become all emotional, particularly if you have lived life in your head for most of your life, shutting out your emotions. However, it will make you more aware of them and the messages they have for you, also known as Emotional Intelligence. Yes, it may be uncomfortable for a time when working on them yourself, the exercise near the end of this section will be of an enormous value during this phase. But many people prefer to work with someone than to do it alone. If this is you, then see Work with Kim at the end of this book. Where I will detail what you can do to, work directly with me.

By listening to the Unconscious messages of emotions, you can begin to identify what you need to do to repoint your life to one that you want, full of love, joy, freedom, happiness and health. You can begin to understand who you have been, and who you can become. When you apply this knowledge to others around you, you can begin to realise just how much everyone is doing the best they can with what they 'know'. (See the Habits and thinking section on how people 'create' their world).

What Now?

As extreme emotions of hate or love can be somewhat overwhelming – making people feel uncomfortable, awkward, frightened or fearful in probably equal measure, there are a few things to think about when working with your own emotions

Every emotion has a spectrum, at the one end little or no emotion to the other end, extreme emotion You may not be able to clear all the emotion at once, so just realise that you can lessen its impact on you, every time you need to, until it is no longer a problem.

Some emotions are just indescribable by a single word, however, the beauty of the exercise in this section, means you just need to FEEL the emotion to be able to clear it!

Many emotions mask others, particularly if the unconscious does not feel safe in addressing the root cause straightaway. Many people who come to therapy deal mostly with the external world that is causing them issues, and it is only over time, as trust is built, and it becomes louder, are they ready to then face up to the deeper level of emotions. I know this myself. Telling myself I was stressed when, quite frankly I was terrified and anxious. I was not good at expressing emotions easily, living as I did in my head. Stress therefore was covering up for a multitude of other emotions (big and small) that were buried deep in my psyche. Similarly, for you, there may be other emotions underneath the presenting one. When learning NLP (Neuro Linguistic Programming) back in 2004, I was taught that anger was the most obvious, visible emotion that covered up sadness, which covered up fear, which covered up guilt or jealousy. Whether that is true doesn't really matter, it just provides the idea that one emotion can mask the another and how they can be layered

Be kind to yourself with what you feel – it is ok.

If you are full of fear, grief, depression jealousy, or powerlessness, imagine the spectrum within that could be on a scale of 1–10, with 1 being the best it could be or 10 being the worst.

Once you have identified where you are, try and identify what you might be thinking that has resulted in this emotion or what triggers it, (an event, a person or circumstance)? What could you be, do or think, differently that would enable you to improve by at least one point or more? The challenge can be doing this in isolation. I know Anthony Robbins has demonstrated time and time again that it is possible to change our emotional state in a fraction of second. (Check him out on You Tube) and you could too - you simply need to learn how.

Exercise 5: EFT

I have found that EFT is the easiest and most effective way for clearing emotions easily without having to go through lots of self-analysis.

EFT or Emotional Freedom Technique is a powerful way of moving and changing how you feel in the moment, so you don't really need to analyse them too deeply if you prefer not to. The only issue is that you may not clear things up at a root cause, but for addressing the immediate emotion, it is perfect. Rather than describing it here I am going to point you to the expert I turn to. His name is Nick Ortner and his website has some videos explaining how to do it. www.thetappingsolution.com.

I have found this a powerful intervention because the tapping on key points around the head, chest and hands, can 'interrupt' the thought processes that are reflected in the body and vice versa. It does this by firstly engaging your conscious mind. You are repeating in your head or out loud phrased to help you clear the emotional content, the old belief or issue; then you are 'tapping' on key parts of the head, chest and under arm to engage your senses of touch, sight and sound. This engagement of the 3 senses (by all means if you want to add smell by lighting a candle then even better) creates a very powerful way of overriding the old conditioning. This leaves you free to then create a new way of being, seeing and doing that fits more with who you are today. You have interrupted the old pattern or conditioning and replaced it with something more empowering.

In most cases, you will feel some (maybe small) difference in how you feel, if this is not enough, then you continue until it is significantly reduced. If, however, you do not immediately notice an improvement in how you feel, either because nothing seems to have changed feeling wise (but you are now changing your thoughts) or because it has been replaced by another unwanted emotion. You are not doing it wrong, it is about continuing with the process. It really is about practice, practice, practice and the more you do this, the easier it becomes and the easier it becomes, the faster it can provide real change.

Gradually you can begin to move up the emotional scale as you clear old stuff.

What If the Event Is Too Emotional or Not Clearing?

Sometimes an event is so emotional that you feel that you could be overwhelmed by it. I would strongly recommend you seek help from a qualified professional to help guide you through the process. Know that everyone needs help from time to time (you see a doctor when you are not well, a plumber when you have a leak, a financial advisor for a mortgage, why not a therapist when you have something going on?) imagine coming out stronger for it. And if your conditioning has you feeling shame because you need help, then you definitely need to see one! If you believe you 'should' be able to deal with it yourself, how is that, when you have not been shown how? I have only been in a position to write this book because I was able to get help from counsellors, courses, various therapists and friends.

Remember any resistance to getting help or doing the work successfully yourself, is just that your Unconscious is protecting you and it may need more reassurance that you will be okay. A bit like a child who doesn't want to let go of their parents when going to school for the first time – change can be frightening and change can mean being vulnerable.

Acknowledging emotions that you have kept locked up, in itself can be just enough. But working through them is a key part of caring for ourselves and our physical bodies.

3rd Key: Thinking

Faulty Thinking

Hopefully as you are working through this

book, you are beginning to see how your beliefs, values and emotions are already driving much of what you are thinking – and you thought you were in control!

As shown earlier in the book, much of your thinking will have been picked up from your early years and is constantly being refined with each new piece of information.

Like emotions in the previous section this is not about positive or negative thinking, it is about identifying the signposts to the next level of learning.

I mentioned earlier, how I liken the way the brain works to a computer storing more and more data so that it begins to slow and if you load other software programmes, they are sometimes incompatible. The security which is protecting you from the harmful worms and viruses that are out there, may also be preventing you from carrying out the simplest operation.

It is worth exploring briefly how thought comes about. I have mentioned that our senses pick up information from our outside world and pass this back into our inner world via the brain. Simply put, the messages are relayed back via the limbic system which plays a vital role in perception, interpretation and response to those signals. (For more information, Google Thalamus, Amygdala, Hippocampus and Hypothalamus) The limbic system is then responsible for processing emotions as well as storing memories and creating new ones.

This response is processed so quickly, it

precedes any Conscious thought stored in a different part of the brain. By the time our Conscious mind is aware, the brain has already decided on an initial course of action based on stored information, but we think it is our doing.

If you do not realise that decisions are made in advance of Conscious thinking, what can you do about it? Well, there are a few thought habits that might be going on that you can start to pay attention to that have led to Faulty Thinking. Faulty Thinking is a great guide to let you know what is going on and include:

Models of the World

There is an idea that if you repeat something often enough you can learn it. If you learn it, it can become a habit which eventually becomes a rule (belief), which then drives your thinking and eventually when repeated enough, becomes who you are.

Once this happens, your Unconscious mind starts to filter your world according to these rules, your values and attached emotions, thus creating your own version of a 'model of the world'. The trouble with a model is that it restricts everything else that does not fit into that model.

For example, remember when it was believed the world was flat? Or that cigarettes were essential for looking cool? Everyone buys into concepts like this all the time and then they become absorbed into their model of the world and they play them out. What is a Model of the World? It is a way of believing, thinking, responding and experiencing the world as you have learnt it and defined it. An example might be buying a yellow car. Up until then you have barely noticed any other yellow cars, but all of a sudden you are seeing them everywhere! Your model of the world has just opened up to include yellow cars! Or suddenly a piece of information you have always 'known' about suddenly takes on more meaning, for example, loving yourself, may have sounded like a platitude in the past, but for some reason, you can suddenly see how you can do this in a way that is right for you. Your model of the world has just opened up! Can you begin to see now how you might just have re-created your life? Your experiences? Your outcomes? By being completely unaware of what else is going on around you because your unconscious had been 'closed' to it?

The key way your models are challenged so that you can look objectively at them is; if someone questions something you have always taken as true about you, the model no longer seems to be providing you the right experiences, and life has become hard or boring; you meet someone who inspires you and you see life from a different viewpoint. What if you could do this for yourself though? Earlier we have looked at your beliefs, values and emotions as pointers to anything in your world that is or isn't working for you. And your thoughts can do this too. When you have a thought about something, begin to notice the thought itself, ask the question "what is that about?"; Is that True?"; "is that the only way?"

By learning to question what goes through your head, you can then open up your perspective and see opportunities that were probably always there, but filtered out and can now be presented to you because your Unconscious can be open to it.

Over Thinking

Many people find they are unable to turn off their thinking at the end of the day. Thoughts are rattling around like a toy train on a circular track and nothing seems to quieten them.

Or perhaps you are one of those people whose thinking is about everything that could go wrong, constantly analyzing and assessing 'what if', but there can be so many permutations you can give yourself a headache thinking about it!

These never-ending thoughts can become debilitating and I have noticed how people who experience anxiety seem to be particularly prone, as they are fearful of people, events, situations and their Unconscious mind cannot hope to cater for all the possibilities of what might happen. This can leave them feeling anxious, overwhelmed and out of control.

One of the best things for this sort of conditioning is to start to recognise the thinking and understand what is behind it using the belief and emotion sections to help you. It is important to always look at the emotional content as this will be an additional trigger to make any anxiety, fear or worry worse. Once you have got to the root of the thought, via that emotion and belief, you are then able to clear it (see exercises under each section) and make way for adding in more powerful beliefs. One of the things I have found with faulty thinking is that the thoughts are a jumble and interweave with each other. It can be complex, and you may only be able to do so a little at a time, but the more you clear the emotional content and old beliefs, the easier your thoughts can become.

Have patience. As you unpick each one, eventually you will see that the old thought patterns are beginning to subside and you can replace them.

Another way to interrupt the cycle of thoughts is the Automatic Writing exercise (Exercise 1 Inner Search) to bring out what is going on for you. This can be a powerful exercise to do just before bed, particularly if your thoughts keep you awake at night. It gives you the chance to 'air' your thoughts, whilst downloading so that you do not have to hold onto them. I have found that asking a question as you go to be, can result in an answer the next morning! (Sometimes might take a few days, but it does happen!)

I have found that those who experience this faulty thinking are not always aware of the emotional content that is running at the same time, somehow it has become detached. That is ok. In the tapping exercise in the Emotions Section you can use this to get a sense of what is going on for you and that technique can still help! The actual content does not have to be known. For example, you could say "all these unhelpful thoughts" or all these "unwanted thoughts".

Inner Critic

Some people have difficulties because of their Inner Critic – a voice constantly judging and telling them what they are doing wrong, identifying all their shortcomings

This can eventually lead people to stop trying, (refer to the Models of the World section about being what you think) eventually believing that they are not good enough, not important enough, enough is never enough etc. Alternatively, working themselves into the ground by being perfectionists in everything they do, trying harder and harder. Some people may be completely unaware that this inner voice is there, having been there since childhood, it has become normalised. The harsher the childhood, the harsher the critic.

By working on the exercises in this book and becoming aware of what you are thinking, you can begin to recognise this inner critic. It will never say anything good about you! Until you understand that it is actually attempting to protect you in some way, from failure, from ridicule, from judgement, then you can begin to understand how you can address this, imagine how powerful that would be!

Habitual Thinking

Unlike faulty thinking and inner critic thinking, this is just the thinking that you do all the time.

That you 'have to' have a morning coffee; that you 'must' clean the house before going on holiday; that you 'should' see your parents more. Habitual thinking also includes the phrases you tell yourself frequently "I am fat", "I hate socialising", "my job is stressful" and before you know it, your Unconscious has listened and like the genie in the lamp, it obeys your wishes. It is vital that you identify what you want to think! Which is challenging when most of what you think is habitual!

My advice is to notice what you notice and focus on one unhelpful thought at a time! To do this, notice your language, as these will be indicators. Which of these are in your vocabulary? Notice how they feel when you use them. Does it feel heavy, difficult, negative, reluctant?

❖ I must

❖ I should

❖ I can't

❖ I have to

❖ I ought to

Begin to replace these with more empowering different language such as I can, I want to, I choose to, I love to. Before long you will begin to see this is your new go to phrase and you just might notice how things seem easier.

This may have to be more Conscious to start with, but you can soon start to spot them all! As you make changes to your thinking you can begin to really notice how your world and the universe begin to reorganise to deliver you different results!

Other Options to Change Thinking

Learning

Start researching thinking patterns by looking at the likes of Dr Joe Dispenza, Dr Deepak Chopra or Dr David Hamilton – all of them talk about how you can change yourself. Or follow what interests you. Go wherever your curiosity takes you, a course, a book, a video, a destination. Each one you follow will lead you to where you really want to be, doing what you really love. Opening up your world and changing what you thought you knew.

By learning and being open to new ideas, viewpoints, philosophies and weighing them against what you already know, you will find what works for you. Not everything they say will resonate, so go and find something, someone or somewhere that does. This wonderful tool called the internet has much good to offer – you just have to start looking.

As you start to open yourself up to new ways of being, incorporating what is right for you, your life will gradually take a new path, the old one fading into the background the more you practice.

Learning new concepts of how to re-create your reality is a much more empowering way to view the world and all it takes is making a choice of being more open to the new, the different, the challenging.

Mindfulness & Meditation

Listening to your heart/Unconscious can lead you onto a very different path than the one you are already on, it could be wholly better in so many ways

One way to understand the Heart/Unconscious connection is through the practice of mindfulness. This is about awareness of what you are doing, feeling and thinking in the now. Once you become aware, you become really present truly in the now, begin to notice any colours, sounds, smells or all senses at once that are being engaged. Is it pleasurable, or distasteful? By really paying attention, you can become more aware of what is going on for you in any one minute. Mindfulness can be practiced at any time; when you are in a meeting, when washing up etc., because it is the other things that distract you, that mean you are not fully present.

Meditation can also be done at any time, but not recommended when you are driving or undertaking tasks that require your full attention. Here your attention is drawn inwards, towards what is going on in your head, your body and your heart. Just listening to what they are all telling you; the ache in your back, the reoccurring or long forgotten memory, emptiness in the heart area - so many different things for different people. "Whatever arises, love that" (Matt Khan) is a saying I think should be used whenever something is discovered that is not to our liking. Remember, it was taken on at a time when you did not know better, and has served you – until now.

I used to go along to a meditation session run by a lovely Buddhist monk, where there were only two meditations – Mindfulness of Breathing and Loving Kindness. I thought I would get bored with just two – my mind craved difference. But I learned how much each meditation could be different and bring different things to me. Even as I write this, I am thinking I need to get back to it!

You can see how by noticing your thinking, you could begin to really impact your reality. But like all good things it will require some effort, time to adjust and time for your Unconscious mind or Universe to deliver what it is you are now thinking and believing

Volunteering

One other way you can begin to change your thinking is by looking at volunteering. There is nothing like helping others to help put your life in perspective. I have started a Carers Support Group on Facebook. I am not a carer, but I have a few in the family who have been, and I have seen the toll it can take on people. It is something I do in my spare time, but it would be fabulous if I can bring a little bit of light to people's lives when they are struggling. It takes may be a couple of hours a week, you choose how much time works for you. My one word of caution on this though, is that you ensure that you are able to say no. As a volunteer, it can be easy to find yourself saying yes too often!

4th Key: Habits/Behaviours

There are at least 4 reasons people create habits:

To Fit In

Humans are social animals who want to be in groups and as such to be 'part of the tribe' can mean that people end up doing what is the norm, regardless of whether they agree or not. This is because in the past, you ran the risk of being permanently excluded or finding yourself in peril from other tribes and predators. Nowadays it is about fitting into friendship groups as a teenager, work colleagues or social groups as an adult. Everyone wants to belong somewhere and feel part of something.

To Be Safe

Humans are ultimately driven by their Unconscious to keep safe.

When the limbic system is triggered, logic can go out of the window. You may not know this, but you cannot be logical and emotional at the same time. The emotional brain will always win out, as it is trying to keep you safe... always. If it has been activated, it is all about reacting fast, not thinking!

Where once it was keeping you safe from predators, now it is keeping you safe from the new 21st century predators. Such as the angry shopper, the demanding boss, the final demands, the aggressive driver the depressed partner, the challenging parents. The Unconscious doesn't know what the risk is, just that you are under threat from somewhere or someone.

To ensure that it can do this effectively, the Unconscious is always looking for ways to do things better and easier to free up time for its primary objective, keeping you safe. One of the ways it does this is through habits. At any one moment, you are being bombarded with information from our world and habits are a way of automating things to reserve space for all these myriads of things going on. The habit is just like a production line, keeping everything working just as it should; doing all the small, repetitive things automatically and repeatedly every day.

A habit can lead you to live your live in a trance like state. Have you ever driven a car and realised the last 5 miles passed by and you can't remember? Or found time flying by because you got lost in the music?

Modelled from Others

It is the small things that you do every day that contribute and build your model of the world. Remember as a child being taught to clean your teeth before bedtime and when you got up in the morning? That sort of early conditioning sets up your fundamental habits.

These might have been absolutely right at the time, but are they right, for right now?

Habits are evidence of the way your Unconscious has learnt something that made life easy and which may not be your own! A habit can be considered a thought that is repeated often until the brain has learnt in order to respond to cues automatically, without Conscious thinking.

For example, you may have learned as a child that when things got tough you turned to food or drink for consolation. How many of us were bought sweets when they fell over? Or as an adult had a cup of tea when things were tough? Or learned that to fit in with a crowd during their teenage years, they had to smoke? Just 3 examples of where the habit was someone else's but you learned it all the same.

I want to share a story to show another example of how habits can be passed down the generations.

The Newlywed

There was once a young newlywed couple who were getting ready to cook a Sunday roast. As the husband prepared the vegetables, the wife prepared the meat. They were having roast beef, a favourite for them both.

The wife took the beef and set about cutting off either end before wrapping and putting in the oven. "Why did you do that?" asked the husband. "Why did I do what?" answered the puzzled wife. "Cut off the end of the beef" said the husband

"Because that is the way I was taught to do it" she answered.

This puzzled the husband so when they were next at his mother in law's, he asked the same question of her. "Why do you cut off the end of the beef?" The mother turned and smiled gently at him, "because that was the way I was taught by my mother" she said.

"Hmmm" thought the husband, still not really understanding.

When the following week they had the opportunity to see the grandmother, he took the opportunity to ask her too – "why do you cut off the end of the beef?"

The Grandmother threw her head back and laughed out loud! "Oh, my dear boy! It goes back to when I was a young mum with several mouths to feed. I only had a small oven, and most joints would not fit in, so I had to cut them to size!"

At last he had found out that actually it had been a practical solution to a problem of the size of the oven for the grandmother, but the mother had clearly watched and learned (as does everyone) and she had passed that onto her daughter without really questioning what she was doing!

What might you be doing without thinking or questioning?

Managing Time

Another word for habit is routine. Routines start from a well-intentioned place, but they tend to be limited to the time that they are created, so that when something changes they may no longer work. The best example of this is with a new baby. You work to develop a routine with your new baby and just as you find what works for you both, the baby grows and you have to change it!

If you are not careful, like the baby scenario, you will not immediately look at changing the routine – because it was working, right? You keep doing them in the same way, because they worked before.

Your Habits

What do you do automatically without thinking? According to James Clear, all habits have 3 things in common:

- ❖ Reminder – the trigger for the habit to start;
- ❖ Routine – the habit acted out;
- ❖ Reward – What you gain from it.

To start with you may only notice the habit, not the trigger, but this is where finding it is so important for you make better choices.

What habits do you have? The easiest place to look are New Year's Resolution or some goal you set yourself that you did not achieve – what got in the way? What excuses or reasons stopped you? And what did you do instead?

What was the 'normal' behaviour you returned to because it was comfortable and easy?

Some habits will be very supportive, whilst others ones will potentially waste your time and energy whilst not positively contributing to your life.

Habits can be insidious and creep up on you as well. Having just one cream cake once a month is fine; and then you think once a week will be fine, and before you know it, it is daily!

Exercise 6: Habits to Change

According to Adele Du Rand there are 4 questions that can help you identify a bad habit:

❖ What are you doing on a regular basis that may not be supporting you?

❖ What are you doing that makes you cross or guilty about yourself?

❖ What do you do that makes you feel embarrassed to admit to?

❖ What do you do or say that has a negative impact on you or those around you?

To help you here are some common bad habits:

❖ Criticising others
❖ Gossiping
❖ Worrying
❖ Insomnia*
❖ Compulsive behaviours
❖ Overspending/
❖ Getting angry/sad/guilty regularly
❖ Prescription drugs (or the illegal kind)
❖ Drinking
❖ Overeating

❖ Bite, scratch, or pick things?

❖ Always late/very punctual?

*Insomnia becomes a habit when a few sleepless nights become regular, and expectations are that sleeping is elusive

Look at what you do every day, what habits are working for you? Your life is constantly evolving and sometimes your habits and behaviours have to evolve too. Use the earlier exercises to understand what is really going on and see later in the book for how to make the changes you want.

5TH Key – Outcomes

You have already explored what your outcomes have been earlier in Exercise 2 – Life Audit in Chapter 3 on Perceptions. Here you will have listed what outcomes you are currently seeing.

Later in this book, in Chapter 5, you will start to explore in more detail the outcomes you want instead.

SECTION SUMMARY

In this section you have learnt: -

❖ How beliefs are developed and what you can do about developing better ones

❖ How values help drive your choices based on what is important to you and how to identify them

❖ How powerful emotions can be, as your own internal Sat Nav and what you can do to release them

❖ That there are a number of faulty thinking patterns everyone falls into, and how they can be addressed

❖ Learnt the power of habits and how to utilize them to make changes in our world

CHAPTER 5
OPPORTUNITIES

Now that you have identified and started working on what is not working for you, (have you been doing the exercises?) it is time to set up new strategies that can begin to support the new you.

I mentioned that today you are a product of your past. As of today, you are beginning to create a new past to take into tomorrow, one step at a time.

Earlier in the book I mentioned that you are constantly getting whispers, signs and emotions that guide you for what is not working, but also what is!

Maybe you are drawn into a book shop or get a sudden urge to ring a friend. You have no idea why and then something happens that is positive - something you needed to hear or see. The work you have done will enable you to make sure every choice, every decision is taking you towards a better, brighter future and the beauty of this is that you are in control.

This book is about people taking back control of their lives and starting to live the life they have dreamed of. As a friend once said to me, doing more of what you love and less of what you don't, which means following those sudden whims, desires or impulses (with care of course). But make sure it is not a limiting belief leading you astray!

This is not saying you will go from where you are today, to where you want to be overnight, although that has been known to happen for some. It is about setting up a new life structure that will support you to start to move towards it. The beauty of this is that the more you move towards your dream the faster it can come.

What Would You Like?

Once you start thinking and dreaming about possibilities, why not allow yourself to dream more, dream big! There is a saying that if you reach for the stars, and you only get to the moon, you are already further than if you had not reached at all! (Well maybe not quite like that, but I prefer it!)

The question to ask yourself would be; what if you had nothing holding you back? No money worries? No health issues? No responsibilities or constraints? What sort of future would you want?

Allow yourself to dream when you next get 5 minutes on your own over a cup of coffee or when you are in the shower. What do you want, when do you want it, (no guarantees) how do you want it? If you didn't feel obligated, responsible, worrying about others judging or criticising you – what would you do?

Again, this is not to say that you will suddenly abandon your life or the people in it, but what I am looking for here is how you will feel, your emotional response once you get it. Just imagine what would be going on around you, what you would look like, how you be talking and walking, what you would be hearing that lets you know you have succeeded, maybe anything you can smell in the air or taste. Really close your eyes and get a sense of how it feels and notice where that is. This is the feeling I want you to practice, daily! To remind your unconscious what it is, it needs to do, to help you the most!

Make sure you put yourself in the right space first - to dream BIG – to ask yourself "What if" questions!!

Just dream..... what if you could:

* ❖ Create or Re-awaken and rediscover your hopes, dreams and ambitions?
* ❖ Pick up activities or hobbies that you used to love but gave up or didn't pursue?
* ❖ Re-energise yourself?
* ❖ Rediscover or reclaim what happiness means for you?
* ❖ Connect with what brings you joy, love and happiness?
* ❖ Really begin to truly live?
* ❖ Put your needs first to build the health that you deserve?

Putting yourself first is very often viewed as being selfish. But is that really true? What if you looked at it more as 'self–ish', i.e. looking after your needs first, before you make commitments that actually detract, drain, devalue you. If you are in good space, you will be able to help and give to others more effectively and they will notice. If only loving ourselves, nurturing ourselves, caring for ourselves, were encouraged more, then we could begin to attract in more of the same. (Remember your unconscious mind does not like to be wrong).

It is a tough exercise for some people to think about what they really want. I know I struggled with it, as I didn't really know what brought me joy or happiness, my life having been made up of so many beliefs and other peoples wants and desires I had lost who I was.

One tip to help is to think of the young you; what interested or excited you? Some of my early fond memories is of by being near the sea and I love being near water today, so it is on the list!

What were you excellent at? Everyone has gifts, things they did well and many tend to take their skills for granted as they live with them every day, just assuming that everyone else can do them. If you are not sure, ask your family or friends when they saw you at your happiest?

There was a reason you gravitated towards certain things. As a child, you were operating at a purely emotional level doing what made you happy (the logical brain is not fully developed until about the age of 7 or 8). Is there a way that you can begin to bring this experience or activity back into your life more? Perhaps you could re-develop your love of that skill/topic through on-line courses, adult education classes, reading about it, attending groups, speaking to others etc.

You do this by trusting yourself to see where it may lead you, by reviving and reaffirming your native 'intelligence'. You may find it no longer works for you but at least you can say for sure and that frees you up to search for something else.

As you work through these exercises, as you take stock, realise how far you have come and how much further you can really go. There is a Chinese proverb I love which says "there are two occasions to plant the seed of your life, one was the past, and the second is today.

Exercise 7: Your Future Now

There are a number of exercises that you can do that will help you visualise the future and I will use the most common one here for those who may not be aware of it.

The Vision Board

This is where you collect pictures that represent everything you want in your future and put them in one place so that you can see them every day and know what you are working towards.

I tend to do it on my computer and pick pictures from the internet. I currently have two on the go!

I also write short term goals and print them so that I can see them every day, to remind myself what I am aiming for. In the results section I talk about a 90-day Action Plan, where you set yourself short term goals as sometimes it is difficult to make the leap from where you are now to your dreams.

Think about everything you would like to have, where you would like to be, where you live, which car you drive, the money you earn, the health and fitness you have, the social network you have, and what you are doing with your days. What would you be doing on the average day as this new you? Once you have enjoyed that creativity, it is important to make sure that you head, heart and body are all aligned. To do this, look at each item on your list and rate each one out of 10, with 0 not aligned, and 10 raring to make those changes – where do I start??

If under 7, there is more work to be done on clearing blocks i.e. the emotional, physical and mental bodies. This you can do now, by revisiting the exercises earlier in this book. I found this quite powerful when I was working on my physical being, the last thing that was really holding me back.

Letter Writing

Another useful tool is letter writing. It is a variant on the Automatic Writing you did earlier in the book, except now you write a letter to yourself, as though you were in this ideal future you have created, writing back to you now. I have done this from time to time to help encourage and motivate myself. Sometimes it is 5 years ahead and sometimes just months, you pick what you need right now.

Imagine you are coming to the end of your life and you look back over the years. Let your present self know how well they have done, what they have achieved, where they are in life, how they are feeling etc.

- ❖ What advice would you give the current you now?
- ❖ What could you say about the things that are stopping them?
- ❖ What could you say about the many strengths they have?
- ❖ What decisions do they need to make?
- ❖ Which one person will always be there for them, no matter what?
- ❖ Which one person is not good for them, and they need to interact with less and less?
- ❖ What would you like to have done with your life?
- ❖ Where would you like to have visited?
- ❖ What was the most adventurous thing you did that you were proud of?
- ❖ What would your friends and family say about you that would make you feel loved?
- ❖ What was the one thing you did that you were most grateful for?
- ❖ What one thing did you do, that led to the biggest change?
- ❖ Confirm what they have achieved
- ❖ Confirm how they have felt (Loved,

peaceful, happy).

❖ Encourage them in whatever way they need to hear it now.

❖ Confirm they are okay – everything happens for a reason and they are stronger than they know.

I have also used this technique to work on my yearly goals, writing to myself to praise how well I did.

Does it work? Yes, it can! What you are doing is telling your Unconscious a story, what it is you want, and provided there are no blocks it will move you towards it, by bringing into your awareness the things you want. However, let me be clear, this will not bring you fame and fortune overnight or necessarily within a year. It might of course, but in most cases, it does not. It will provide the clues that can take you on the path to that fame and fortune, but you have to do whatever it takes to get there. And this is where most people give up. They do not have the courage to take the tough decisions, or believe in themselves enough to go for what they want. They may be all fired up and on the way, and a setback comes along which triggers an old memory and they stop. What they want doesn't happen fast enough, so they change what they want. It took me over 10 years to get the car of my dreams, and just under 5 to get a small property by the sea. The property however did not turn out to be mine, but I had a part in its purchase, whereas my own home took 10 years. Rather than deflate you, I want you to know that I do things VERY slowly, an old resistance pattern of mine, I will happily chat about over a coffee sometime. Imagine what you could do if you set your mind to something?

Do it with the love of wanting something better and if does not turn out exactly as you expected, you will still be further forwards. Shoot for the stars and if you only get to the moon, then that is good.

So hopefully now you have a vision of the life you would like to have, where you would like to be, where you live, which car you drive, the money you earn, the health and fitness you have, the social network you have and what you are doing with your days.

You may remember that in Exercise 2 (Your Life Audit) you had different areas of your life and you rated them.

Now I want you to compare where you are now with where you want to be and put in your new goals. Write in the last column where you want to be.

For those of you who do not like goals, I use the word intentions because it allows for life to take you where you want to be, and your conscious mind might not yet know where that is! Goals are great for those who are motivated or clear about what they want, but for many people, they can be just another pressure which, if not met, can lead to feelings of failure, being demoralized or disheartened. Life has a funny way of sending through the odd curve ball in life to send you off track! If it is an intention you have set and not a goal, and you didn't achieve it, your critical voice has less to complain about!

Remember, this is about changing (potentially long standing) emotions, thoughts, and habits and it can be a little challenging, so be kind and patient to yourself. This is a life change so it may be more so – the key is to recognize and accept that it will not be perfect all the time! You have your eye on the long game, the better life, the better you, you want so much more than before!

Later, in the Planning section of this book, I help you to plan for the unexpected, the delays, the changes that inevitably come about, so be sure to check that out!

You may believe right now that being promoted is the new best intention but what if does not come about? You feel disappointed and deflated. First of all, remember you set it as an intention not a goal which is just a 'must' in disguise. You are not a magician, you are not able to control all events that happen in your world, so be kind to yourself. The work you are doing is not about retaining control, but learning to ride the waves, cope with all types of weather, and build resilience in the face of adversity. You now know (from earlier in the book, that everything that happens to you, is a message – either a confirmation of what is good or a message that something needs to change) there was probably something to learn and you now know how to use some of the exercises in this book to find out what it was.

Once you understand what happened (perhaps the promotion would have been a detour of your life) you can start opening yourself up for better outcomes.

So, choosing one area of life that needs the most focus, complete the last column with your desired state and make it as detailed as possible, using specifics.

There may be more than one area but focus on one. As you start to make the changes, you may find others will improve anyway!

Life Area	Rating 1-10	Reason for the Rating	New Intention
Self-care	*2*	*I am overweight and I don't exercise.* *I come last on my list.*	*I am at my ideal (state specifics) weight for me and I exercise for 30 minutes every day that enable me to have energy for everything I want to do and be*
Family	*8*	*I have a close and supportive family.*	
Love			

Life Area	Rating 1-10	Reason for the Rating	New Intention
Health & exercise			
Finances			
Vocation or Work			
Social/Fun			
Spiritual			
Contribution or giving back			
Learning, education or broadening horizons			

Life Area	Rating 1-10	Reason for the Rating	New Intention
Other			

Once you have completed this exercise, it will be used again in the Response-ability section for the 90 Day Action Plan to start you moving towards your intentions.

The Power of The Right Energy, Motivation and Your Big WHY

You now know what you want. Once you have completed the 90 Day Action Plan a little later in this book, you will know how you are going to get there. But life WILL get in the way, without a doubt. Someone, maybe you, will be poorly, a sudden deadline at work, somebody needs your help. A myriad of things that can get in your way. As a Programme and Project Manager in a former life, I know the value of preparing for all eventualities. You will not capture all the reasons you don't do something, immediately but there are some broad headings here to get you started. The key is to identify what usually stops you, and start to build alternative behaviours. This won't necessarily immediately make an impact, as you need to repeat the new behaviour for it to become a habit, so all you need is a willingness to accept and move on!

Because motivation may not be enough to see you though.

Motivation is actually a temporary state. Everyone can be motivated for a while, possibly even for months, but it requires energy to keep it going and this is where your BIG WHY comes in.

You know what I am talking about; you were about to go to the gym after a long hard day at work and even though you didn't want to, it was on your way. But out of the blue and old friend is in town for one night only and wants to get together. Before you know it, the gym is past history because family and friends are more important to you on your values list than looking after yourself!

Your BIG WHY dictates what you do and the priority it takes. If what you want to change does not match your values, you may find it harder to achieve, although not impossible. Motivation then may not be enough to see you through until the change becomes normalised, at a head, heart and physiological level.

- ❖ So how do you make it important for you?
- ❖ Why is the change so important to you?
- ❖ How do you make it a priority in life?
- ❖ How do you make time for it?
- ❖ How do you create a state of wanting it and moving towards it?

Are you one of those people who just get on and does it? If you are, how successful have you been in the past? Are you burnt out really quickly (New Year Resolutions?) and then go back to your old ways berating yourself "I didn't want to do it anyway", "It doesn't work for me", get despondent, "I am a failure" or something similar?

STOP!

You might be one of those people who starts things and does really well and then something comes along to break the new habit and that is it! It takes months to get back in the right frame of mind.

STOP!

It might be that you have to be in the right frame of mind to start changing, procrastinating and putting it off. "I will start the diet on Monday", "I will join the gym next month", "I will do it, when I have enough money". Constantly delaying the start as you are not yet committed to the change and planning to do it on the 32nd of never.

STOP!

If like me you have done all of these (and others – do please let me know!) then STOP is exactly what you need to do.

I am a big fan of James Clear who talks about changing habits – check him out at https://jamesclear.com and he talks about the principle of small gains, where you make small to micro changes every day to build up the habit muscle.

For me, the one way to ensure that a change is actually made is by making them SMALL and manageable. Yes, it may take longer, but the change tends to stick and this is in no small part because you are under the radar of the Inner Critic and any limiting beliefs or emotional content of what you are doing. It is so small, it is not scary, and even you would not be able to proffer an excuse worthy of not doing something! The smaller the better because once that small change becomes normalised, you can do the next thing and then the next and then the next and before you know it, over a few weeks or months, you will have noticed the change you wanted coming about. The best bit is that the effort is so small – it is almost bloomin' easy! I like easy! It gives me time to focus on what I want to do! Here are some examples:

Exercising

Please note that this is one area, I have had some miserable success. I go through a period of (usually) about 6 weeks, really inspired to exercise, and then something happens and I stop, usually illness or injury. My plan was to set a small target of moving for 15 mins consecutively every day. However, I have found that even this is not always achievable as I am easily distracted with work or doing the things I love (writing, research and reading). I have changed it to 10 mins. Once I have cemented the habit of movement of 10 minutes at a time, of some intensity, I will then up it to 15 minutes. You will notice I am not prescriptive about what the movement is yet, it is purely about movement. When I am at home, I can walk to the shops and back (10 minutes there, and 10 minutes back); when I am at home, I can walk up the stairs and down a few times. Not only is achievable but I can do something I love whilst doing it (listening to Audible) and it is not so intrusive that it can't be done.

I can build it up in small increments until an inner desire to do more takes over and I am fit enough to do all the things I used to love, swimming, dancing, cycling etc. I am heading in the right direction.

However, I am going to be honest with you at the time of writing this book, I have been recovering from burn out and glandular fever, so not much is happening! I am prepared to be held to account on this!

Eating

Again, I am not your best role model in this area either! But I have included this, because my biggest struggle, is something that others will also understand. I emotionally eat! I have known that for years and have not had the motivation to do anything about it. Until life has taught me I have no choice! I eat because I don't want to do what I have to do, I eat when I am tired, and I eat when I need comfort because I have been stressed, feeling sorry for myself or had a bad day. I will keep this short, as you are probably fully aware of what a good healthy diet is! However, I would like to share my learnings around the whole food thing.

Firstly, just identify the foods you know are not good for you. The ones that you eat most, the ones that make you feel tired or bloated, make you feel bilious or sick and look for alternatives. Do this slowly if you need to, replace that food once a week, then twice a week, then three times a week and so on. Until before you know it, your taste buds will have changed, you will enjoy the replacement and you can start on the next thing.

Secondly, do not believe what you are told by the advertising and marketing guys, they are selling a product! Low fat, low sugar, low salt, products, may well be, but to keep taste, they will bulk it up in another area. For reduced sugar, check the fat. It is better to have the normal produce and just cut back on how much you use.

Thirdly – provided you are not allergic or intolerant, a little of what you love does you good! Practice moderation in all things. Be kind and if you do have something that was once on your 'naughty' list, just realise that it is ok once in a while!

And finally, the best until last, learn to listen to what your body is telling you. It does take effort to notice what it is telling you, whether what you are eating and drinking works for you, but it means you take back control over your body. We do not do this enough, check in for any aches, pains, discomfort and then look at what you have done to contribute to this. If we were taught this early on, people would be able to realise how they were probably part of their issue or at the very least, be able to correct it sooner.

Procrastination

If motivation is the way of getting things done, then procrastination has to be the polar opposite!

I am very good at this – why do today what you can put off until tomorrow! I have no idea where that comes from specifically (although now may be a good time to sort it out!).

Of course, everyone does it and the fact that they do is not really the issue. It is the length of time that they do it, particularly for the things that really matter.

So why do people avoid tasks? Here are some of the reasons:

❖ Not knowing where to start.

❖ Fear they might get things wrong.

❖ Fear they will only succeed in creating a whole set of other issues.

❖ Worry they can't do it/it's too difficult.

❖ Worry the task is too complex and they don't have the skills/knowledge.

❖ Too much effort/can't be bothered.

❖ Don't like it/don't want to do it

The funniest thing is that in order to procrastinate, the individual will find something else to do and keep busy anyway! It is not necessarily a laziness thing. Have you ever heard the term 'busy fool'? Invariably these are the procrastinators who sink their time into email, social media, reading, watching telly, going out with a friend, housework, washing, gym – the list is endless – are you guilty of this? I know I am.

Avoidance is completely natural, thoughts are great at distracting you towards something more exciting (or boring) and where that doesn't work, helping you to 'forget' the task at hand.

Overcoming Procrastination

When the Unconscious brain notices that you are about to do something that might lead you towards fearful places or is out of your comfort zone (even before you Consciously know it), it has already turned away to other, nicer, less important tasks or activities. Sometimes it can be difficult to catch. The trick is how to prepare for the task in hand and overcome the urge to do something else.

1. Create space in your day to do something that you have been putting off, even if this is in two weeks' time, because that way your Unconscious can get used to the idea.

2. Only allocate 5 or 10 minutes to get started. It is said that when exercising the first 5–10 minutes are the hardest as the body adapts to the exercise that you are just about to start. I believe that could be true of all tasks!

3. Remove all distractions. Turn off your phone, email and if there is a likelihood of being interrupted, let people know you

are not to be disturbed.

4. Do the hard tasks first as sometimes these are the things that get in the way.

5. If you find yourself still avoiding, use the EFT technique in the Emotions section to understand what is going on for you and then book some more time in to do another 5 or 10 minutes.

6. Break the task down into much smaller chunks.

7. Consistent and persistent action will get you there in the end! Remember it is not a race.

Gratitude

How many people do you know who seem to focus on what is wrong with their lives and what they don't have? This is one of the most common issues facing people today. Postponing happiness or believing they are going to be a success when they get the next job, next car, bigger house.

They don't recognise all the many things they already have, the people in their life and their life experiences that have helped them 'survive' to this point in time. There are so many people in the world who do not own anything or barely have enough to eat or drink. Whatever you have has to be better than that.

Gratitude, I believe, is an essential ingredient for a happier life. Recognising what you do have, the people you have around you, the money, the home, the fresh drinking water, the food, electricity, safety – so many good things that people tend to take for granted.

Gratitude is one way you can communicate back to the Unconscious more about the things you want.

The Unconscious will then take that message and start to bring your attention to more of that in your world, which means you can be much happier.

For me, gratitude is an energy, an intent about what you love about your life. Even when there doesn't seem much to be happy about, if you woke up this morning, that can be a gratitude start! It means you are breathing and you can be grateful that is one task off your to do list!

An even stronger energy is being appreciative of everything around you. It is a very subtle difference in that gratitude suggest that it comes from a place of lack, whereas appreciation suggests it comes from a place of plenty. Gratitude is a receiving energy, whilst appreciation is more an accumulation energy.

"When people in great numbers choose to practice, integrate, and embody gratitude and appreciation, the cumulative force that is generated can help create the kind of world we all hope for and desire, for ourselves and for future generations" Angeles Arrien, from her book Living in Gratitude: A Journey That Will Change Your Life.

What can you do to improve your world to create more of what you love?

Exercise 8: Gratitude

For the next 28 days, keep a diary of everything that you are grateful for and then repeat. Be mindful of what you notice about how you are feeling, until you begin to enjoy more happiness and peace. For additional help here, check out The Five-Minute Journal as a tool. Check it out on Amazon or www.fiveminutejournal.com

To help you, here is a starter for 10 to think about:

Family	Friends	Partners	Health
Work	Your skills	Your salary	Body
Your home	Utilities	Car	Neighbours
Holidays	Shopping	Nights out	Colleagues
Your body	Your health	Your possessions	A project
Your postman	Emergency services	Council services	Things you can do

When you have done that, go even deeper into each subject, the qualities, the service they provide in your life and how they make you feel etc.

SECTION SUMMARY

In this section, you have begun exploring your future. You have:

❖ Completed exercises to explore and dream big

❖ Understood what is important to you

119

about this future

❖ Learnt how to embrace the right energy that will be important to your success

CHAPTER 6
RESPONSE-ABILITY

You are nearing the end of this book. But it would be remiss of me if I did not take the opportunity to help you a little more.

You now know that: -

❖ You are a product of your past experiences, your beliefs, values, emotions, thoughts and behaviours which may not even be your own.

❖ That when life is not going well, one of these areas is out of balance.

❖ Your beliefs, values, emotions, thinking are your guide, your sat nav to whether you are going in the right direction or not

❖ You can create a better future by clearing out what no longer works for you.

❖ You have a go to toolbox that can help you when you find the imbalance, so that you can let go of old programming.

❖ You have understood the importance of habits and how to change them to support the new you.

In this section, I want to help you take Response–ability to make it happen by introducing my 90-day Action Plan that will enable you to start to drive your life in the direction you want you to take it, plus some useful ways of being that will help you to build upon all the good stuff you are already doing, plus learning to build upon the thinking, emotional and physiological response to your world.

Preparation for Your Future

Using the table in the Opportunities section, it is time to formulate a plan that will enable you to start to identify the smaller steps that will take you from where you are now, to where you want to be.

There are some key points I think it is worth being aware of, that will contribute to your success if you can embrace them. I have already talked about Gratitude/appreciation, so here are some others that will really help.

Forgive Yourself

This is a life change so be prepared to fall off the wagon (so to speak) and find that you are not doing what you wanted or you have not achieved something. According to T Herv Ecker, the chances are you have asked too much of yourself. Make it smaller, shorter, or extend the time! After all you still have a life to live!

Reward Yourself

Many personal development gurus believe everyone should reward themselves for their achievements, they know that this releases endorphins in the body that then make the actions more desirable. Make a list now, of all the many rewards you can give yourself for when you have successfully achieved something. It doesn't have to cost money or be huge – a simple soak in the bath, calling a friend, playing on your PlayStation, going for a run/cycle. Anything is better than nothing! You are sending messages back to your Unconscious that you are worthy!

Consistent and Persistent Action

Even if you cannot achieve everything you set yourself, instantly or in a timescale you have set, this is about setting yourself up for success and telling your unconscious mind what it is you do want! Just one thing every day, perhaps that could contribute to another action, the next step. Whether that is a phone call, research on the internet, writing exercises or just setting some time aside. By consistently doing something every day towards your ideal life, they will come about faster than you realise. Remember if you start today, who knows where you could be in 6 months, 12 months, or 5 years.

The Intent/Goal

As a Programme and Project Manager, I could write oodles on this topic, but to keep it simple, the first thing you need is a draft plan. As you gather information, over time, it will probably change, that is the nature of a plan. It just lets you know where you are in the process, and whether you have deviated. It is a tool to help guide you onto the next step. So be mindful, particularly if you are looking at a big life change, such as moving house, job etc., that you may identify additional steps as time progresses, which will either impact the time, the cost or the quality of what you want. The beauty is that this is your plan, and you can do with it, what you want! Review them at least weekly, but no less than monthly to make sure they are working for you.

Are you ready?

Let's start!

Your Outcome

What is your life outcome? What did you write in the letter back from the future in in the section Opportunities/Letter Writing?

Hopefully, this is the information you have pulled together through this book. And if not, now is the time. You know where are you are now, you have identified what it is you ideally want and you have rated it out of 10 to ensure that you want it enough so that there is nothing obvious stopping you going for it, and you have set it as an intent. This is your future dream.

To make it even stronger and more crystal clear about what it will be like, is to write a typical day in that new life you want. Write it like a diary, from the moment you get up to the moment you go to bed. Think about all the intentions you have put in your Life Audit; how will it feel? What will you be seeing, or hearing? How will your life be different?

Take some time to be really clear about what you are working towards with a laser-like focus. If you are unable to do this, write your outcome the best way you can – you can come back and refine it as often as you like, later as you gain more information.

Think about what your outcome looks like. Who will be part of your outcome? Where will you be? When do you intend to have it? How will you know you have reached it?

Your 5 Year Plan

The next step is to develop a plan to achieve the change, ignore timelines for now, they may restrict your thinking, also imagine money was no object to what you could do. It is about allowing yourself to be creative, to open up to opportunities that perhaps you have not yet seen or heard about, just get sometime mapped out. You can be as sensible as you like a bit later!

Pick just one area you want to improve and identify the initial steps that you believe it will take to get there. People sometimes think there is only one way of doing things (model of the world stuff) but you are not that person anymore and can be open to other ways. For some of you, you will be detailed, for others just a framework, either works, as you work the plan, things will shift, change, be added in or removed!

Once you have written your plan, if like most people, you will have started with the present and worked into the future and that is good.

However, many years ago I had a coach who worked on a plan backwards, a technique that is powerful when looking at what you have to do to achieve what it is you want. It helps identify tasks that might have been forgotten or started to manage your expectations as to whether they are achievable or not. That is not in and of themselves, but whether you are able to commit to them.

He started with a 5-year timeframe, but you choose what works for you.

Outcome Column - Now using the information from the Opportunities section, or your ideal day, transpose or write a high-level summary of your ideal life in 5 years' time into the Outcome column. This is the life you want after all, so miss nothing out. For example:

5 Year Template

Current State	Years					Outcome
	1	**2**	**3**	**4**	**5**	
Self-care						e.g. Regular exercise Massages Holidays
Family						e.g. More time for family fun

	Years					
Current State	**1**	**2**	**3**	**4**	**5**	**Outcome**
Love						e.g. In a reciprocal loving relationship
Health and exercise						
Finances						
Vocation or Work						
Social/Fun						
Spiritual						
Contribution or Giving Back						
Learning or Broadening Horizons						
Other						

5 years' column – In this column, write what will have needed to achieve to get to you where you want to be. Keep it big picture at the moment. Detail can follow later

Do the same for year 4, what would you need to have achieved to meet your year 5 goals?

Continue for year 3, year 2, year 1?

Now you are starting to get a picture of what you need to achieve this next year, in order to be working towards that fabulous you!

How does that compare to your original present to achievement plan? Does it now seem all too real? Achievable? Scary? Whatever it is, it is ok. Be with whatever you are feeling, the unconscious is probably realizing that there is much to do, and feels under pressure, which means you FEEL under pressure. This is why intentions can be much better than goals, as it eases that pressure. Let's continue the process and see where you end up.

Remember this is where the Principle of Small Gains begins to pay off. It is the actions that you do every day that will take you to where you want to be, because they have a compounded effect. These are the existing habits that support you, or the new ones you need to introduce. Yes, just like compounded interest, if you do something every day, you will begin to subtly see things changing for the better!

The more you do, the easier some of the other changes will be to make happen. So now let's move to the 12 Month Template.

12 Month Template

	Months				
Current State	**1-3**	**4-6**	**7-9**	**10-12**	**Outcome**
Self-care					
Family					
Love					
Health and exercise					
Finance					
Vocation or Work					
Social/Fun					
Spiritual					
Contribution or Giving Back					
Learning or Broadening Horizons					
Other					

Now it is time to focus on the next 12 months and follow the same approach. Start at month 12 and write what you would need to achieve in a year, to be on target for your 5-year plan, by the end of year 1.

And then in a similar vein as before, write what you would need to have done to achieve your first-year goals in month 10 -12, what would you need to have done to achieve month 7 -9 and so on.

How is it looking? More or less scary? More or less exciting? Just go with the flow, there will be chance to review it shortly. There is one more step to go.

The 90 Day Plan

In my experience, if a goal/intention is too far out, it can change just as quickly as life does and remaining rigid about the plan could cause you to become overwhelmed, stressed, frustrated or agitated with it. However, this is your plan, and only you will be holding you to account.

This is where I, personally would start to put in real detail in at this level. Most of us know or have a good idea or our existing commitments and have a better idea of being able to define what we can realistically do. With this time frame you can begin to get some real successes under your belt.

This will form your 90 Day (Rolling) Action Plan and you can now become really specific about what you are going to do each week and each day. What do I mean by rolling? This is where you review your 90-day plan regularly (every week or every month whichever works for you) and update it. Some things you will achieve easily, and others may take longer, but as you work through the year, consistently and persistently, things will begin to happen. You may find other things added to the plan, and some fall away, having been found to be unnecessary or no longer required.

It is recommended that you, identify no more than 3 actions per week to begin with that you will do and set time aside to do them, say 1 big task and a couple of small ones. If you are intent on losing weight, may be in the first few weeks, you start with just getting moving as mentioned in the section on exercise and perhaps the big task could be to plan meals for you and family that will enable you to eat more healthily. This is actually much bigger than the first, as you will need to plan, shop, prepare, schedule time in to cook and keep the family happy!

As mentioned earlier, make sure you reward yourself for what you have done. Even just once a week, this is important to do, a phone call with a good friend or a cup of coffee, make sure you have something to look forward to.

Then move onto the next month and so on, until you complete your first 90-day outcome.

Make sure you are happy that they are achievable, by scoring them out of 10 again. With 10 absolutely ready to do it, to 0 highly unlikely. Once again, this is just feedback for you to, to know how committed you are to the work. It need be only for you.

Life has funny way of getting in the way though, so if you have not achieved something, just check in with yourself to see why, as well as check the Overcoming Obstacles section further on in this chapter.

Current State	1 - 15	16 - 30	31 - 45	46 - 60	61 - 75	76 - 90	Outcome
Self-care							
Family							
Love							
Health and exercise							
Finances							
Vocation or work							
Social/ Fun							
Spiritual							
Contribution or Giving Back							
Learning or Broadening Horizons							

Current State	1 - 15	16 - 30	31 - 45	46 - 60	61 - 75	76 - 90	Outcome
Other							

Once you have the next two weeks mapped out, how are you going to ensure you are doing the right things? By writing a daily log. Only this is going to be retrospective at the end of each day or week. Get yourself a notebook and write up what you have achieved, what got in the way, what went well and what didn't. Potentially, this will only be required to get you going in the first few weeks until you start to see the benefits of what you are doing, or for those times when you 'fall off the wagon'.

If you combine this with your gratitude practice you will find, looking back, just how much you have achieved, particularly when the going gets tough, as it naturally will.

I was recently asked to write down everything I had achieved in the past 12 months and I honestly couldn't remember everything. I do keep an (almost) daily journal, so it is just a matter of going back through them and then being surprised at what I had achieved, but I think to review what you have done on a more regular basis could really help you to keep going, keep you motivated.

As you go through this process, you will probably refine your outcomes or even change them. This is okay, sometimes what you want can change as you start the process. Just allow that flexibility if things change.

Obstacles You May Encounter

What might stop you from achieving your goals/intentions? Is it money? People? Technology? Knowledge? Identify what might get in your way and then use some of your new practices to find a solution. You know whether there is an alternative way around it. Trust your inner wisdom – it has gotten you this far!

Use this table as a guide to how to address them!

The Obstacle	What I could do	Who could help?
Time	Schedule time in the diary and only emergencies such as illness get in the way	Partner or friend and ask them beforehand to get their agreement

Time - What is it they say we all have the same amount of time every day as everyone else? Check what is important to you, as perhaps this is playing second to something else. It is your call if that is the case, but remember, you are important in your life too! An hour a week is not much to ask to spend on you.

Money – this usually gets in the way at some point. Either there is not enough or you have not justified it to yourself. If it is lack, what could you do to bring in more income? Can you find a free version of what you need i.e. training course? Alternatively, is there something in your monthly budget you would be willing to let go? I want you to know, that these are not easy decisions, particularly if you have a family, but sometimes it is for their benefit too. I don't know your circumstances, but if you really want to make this change, see how creative you could be! Allow some time for this, money is a big one for everyone, and sometimes it can take a bit of time to move things around!

People – particularly partners who are worried about what you are doing and how it will affect them. Think about how you can include them in your plans? Explain what you are going to do, and that you need their help. If they decide not to be involved, this does not need to stop you, it is about being tactful, respectful and determined that you are still going ahead. Maybe you need the help of someone. Look for people who can support you and help you with whatever it is you need to do.

Technology – this is possibly the easiest to work on. For most people, they are familiar enough with the internet to search for what they want. And there are plenty of training courses on line (You Tube, Udemy on Facebook etc.) that can help. If you are looking at re-training for a different line of work, there is adult education and Open Universities and I know there are grants that you can get if you need help.

Life – sometimes life just gets in the way, and it is wise to allow for this in your planning. You know what I mean, the times when the children are poorly, your partner has to work late, or a social event comes up. Once you write down all the things that may get in your way, identify what you can do about it. Reschedule the time? Find the money elsewhere? Find someone else to help you? You can build on this obstacle list as you progress through the months, and you will find there will be a selection of 'go to' actions you can take. If it is more you getting in your own way (procrastination, motivation etc.) use the tools in this book to get you back on track. There is no failing, only not restarting!

You have got this!

Take your time to play with this, it is better that it is something you are happy with and is achievable for you.

Good luck!

SECTION SUMMARY

In this section, you have learnt:
- ❖ Some supporting habits when times get tough
- ❖ How your outcome helps to formulate a suitable Action Plan
- ❖ The benefits of backward planning from outcome to the present moment to really test what it is you want and whether it is achievable
- ❖ How to manage obstacles that may get in your way and to think about what you will do when they occur

CHAPTER 7
WHAT NEXT?

There was so much that could have been put into this book, but I have covered enough to help you on your way. It is down to you now. Remember; consistent and persistent action will get you where you want to be and you have some tools that will help you to really understand the root cause of what is going on for you when you are not moving in the right direction, rather than the external reasons that everyone else looks to blame.

Even as I have written this book, I have either learned something or been reminded of something that I used to do, so it will always be there for you, when you need it too. In my life, I do not set one goal and that is it. For me this has become a way of life, to become a better and stronger, and more empowered version of me.

I know from personal experience, that books like this can inspire people, but I like a bit of help on the way. I have worked with a few coaches in my time, and the plan you have come up with, could be even better and more achievable as you start to work with them.

If this is you, someone who needs someone to walk beside them, or you are like me and just impatient to get going, why not reach out to me, and book a session. I work via Zoom or Skype, and it would be honour to see how I might be able to help. You already know some of what I will do!

My email address is kim@kimsearle.co.uk and my website is www.kimsearle.co.uk.

As I finish writing this book, know that the changes you make will not only influence your life for the better, but potentially those around you, family, friends or beyond.

The work you do for yourself, becoming your better you, can have so many positive repercussions on those around you and even those future generations to come. The happier, healthier and wealthier you are, you give them permission to be so to. By letting go of old conditioning you can really begin to have a brighter future, being the you that you really want to be. I can't think of a better gift.

But my greatest wish for you is:

❖ A greater self-confidence and self-belief in yourself.

❖ To rediscover your drive and reclaim your happiness

❖ To realise who you really are before life got in the way.

❖ That you become empowered to be more you.

❖ That you have access to a wealth of wisdom that is already in you.

❖ That you express a greater, deeper love for yourself and others.

❖ That your journey be one full of love, laughter, joy, health and happiness.

Thank you

APPENDIX 1
WORK WITH THE AUTHOR

Sometimes with the best will in the world, we may need help. If after reading this you decide you would prefer help because you are: -

❖ Struggling to make the changes

❖ Impatient to get it sorted

❖ Too tired to think

❖ Trusting your judgement less and less

❖ Better working with someone

Then reach out to Kim to see how she can help. Kim has worked with many clients over the years facing a number of different challenges in life. After working with Kim, they have reported: getting promotions, beginning a new relationship, buying their first home, overcoming a fear of success and experienced massive life changes such as working in the corporate arena to moving to distant lands and living a more fulfilling life. What is not to like!

For the majority of people, most see a significant change within 4 – 6 sessions, generally held weekly. How important is it to you to make that change? Is 6 weeks a small price to pay to get you on your way? Contact Kim now to book your first session!

Email: kim@kimsearle.co.uk

APPENDIX 2
RESOURCES

Rhonda Byrne
- ❖ https://www.rhondabyrne.com

James Clear
- ❖ https://jamesclear.com

Dr Joe Dispenza
- ❖ http://www.drjoedispenza.com
- ❖ https://youtu.be/W81CHn4l4AM

Adele Du Rand
- ❖ http://www.adeledurand.com

Gill Edwards
- ❖ http://www.livingmagically.co.uk
- ❖ Living Magically

Dr Bruce Lipton
- ❖ https://www.brucelipton.com
- ❖ The Biology of Belief

Louise L Hay
- ❖ https://www.louisehay.com/about/
- ❖ You Can Heal Your Life

Shakti Gawain
- ❖ http://www.shaktigawain.com/
- ❖ The Path of Transformation – How Healing Ourselves Can Change the World

T Herv Ecker
- ❖ https://www.harveker.com

Daniel Goleman
- ❖ http://www.danielgoleman.info/topics/emotional-intelligence/

Andrew Matthews
- ❖ https://andrewmatthews.com
- ❖ Follow Your Heart – Finding purpose in Your Life and Work

Nick Ortner
- ❖ https://www.thetappingsolution.com
- ❖ https://youtu.be/ZfZBHWSbrsg

Anthony Robbins

https://www.tonyrobbins.com

Trevor Sylvester
- ❖ https://www.trevorsilvester.com/
- ❖ The Question is the Answer

Deepak Chopra
- ❖ https://www.deepakchopra.com
- ❖ Quantum Healing – Exploring the Frontiers of Mind/Body Medicine

Dr David Hamilton
- ❖ http://drdavidhamilton.com

Matt Kahn
- ❖ http://www.truedivinenature.com

Angeles Arrien
- ❖ http://www.angelesarrien.com/
- ❖ Living in Gratitude: A Journey That Will Change Your Life

Kim Searle

ABOUT THE AUTHOR

Kim Searle was born in Hampshire UK, and spent most of her adult life working in the IT & Telecoms sector. Her heart though, has always been with people, providing a shoulder to cry on, a sympathetic ear for those going through tough times in life. It was only after her own life traumas caught up with her, that she went onto qualify as a Cognitive Hypnotherapist, NLP Master Practitioner, Coach and Spiritual Practitioner. Kim is now working for herself and positioning herself as an Emotional Health Guru.

Midlife is NOT a Crisis is her first book, based on the processes she has used with clients and herself to help them heal and let go. Kim has already started work on her next book.

www.kimsearle.co.uk

Printed in Poland
by Amazon Fulfillment
Poland Sp. z o.o., Wrocław